COLLECTED POEMS

1909–1935

by T. S. Eliot

SELECTED ESSAYS: 1917–1932

AFTER STRANGE GODS

MURDER IN THE CATHEDRAL

COLLECTED POEMS

THE ROCK

T. S. ELIOT

COLLECTED
POEMS

1909 - 1935

Harcourt, Brace and Company

New York

This book is complete and unabridged.
It is manufactured in conformity with gov-
ernment regulations for saving paper.

DESIGNED BY ROBERT JOSEPHY
PRINTED IN THE UNITED STATES OF AMERICA

CONTENTS

7

CHORUSES FROM "THE ROCK"

BURNT NORTON

PRUFROCK

AND OTHER OBSERVATIONS
1917

For Jean Verdenal, 1889–1915
mort aux Dardanelles

la quantitate
Puote veder del amor che a te mi scalda,
Quando dismento nostra vanitate
Trattando l'ombre come cosa salda.

THE LOVE SONG
OF J. ALFRED PRUFROCK

S'io credesse che mia risposta fosse
A persona che mai tornasse al mondo,
Questa fiamma staria senza piu scosse.
Ma perciocche giammai di questo fondo
Non torno vivo alcun, s'i'odo il vero,
Senza tema d'infamia ti rispondo.

LET us go then, you and I,
When the evening is spread out against the sky
Like a patient etherised upon a table;
Let us go, through certain half-deserted streets,
The muttering retreats
Of restless nights in one-night cheap hotels
And sawdust restaurants with oyster-shells:
Streets that follow like a tedious argument
Of insidious intent
To lead you to an overwhelming question. . .
Oh, do not ask, "What is it?"
Let us go and make our visit.

In the room the women come and go
Talking of Michelangelo.

The yellow fog that rubs its back upon the window-
    panes,

The yellow smoke that rubs its muzzle on the
    window-panes
Licked its tongue into the corners of the evening,
Lingered upon the pools that stand in drains,
Let fall upon its back the soot that falls from
    chimneys,
Slipped by the terrace, made a sudden leap,
And seeing that it was a soft October night,
Curled once about the house, and fell asleep.

And indeed there will be time
For the yellow smoke that slides along the street,
Rubbing its back upon the window-panes;
There will be time, there will be time
To prepare a face to meet the faces that you meet;
There will be time to murder and create,
And time for all the works and days of hands
That lift and drop a question on your plate;
Time for you and time for me,
And time yet for a hundred indecisions,
And for a hundred visions and revisions,
Before the taking of a toast and tea.

In the room the women come and go
Talking of Michelangelo.

And indeed there will be time
To wonder, "Do I dare?" and, "Do I dare?"
Time to turn back and descend the stair,
With a bald spot in the middle of my hair—
[They will say: "How his hair is growing thin!"]
My morning coat, my collar mounting firmly to the
    chin,
My necktie rich and modest, but asserted by a
    simple pin—
[They will say: "But how his arms and legs are
    thin!"]
Do I dare
Disturb the universe?
In a minute there is time
For decisions and revisions which a minute will
    reverse.

For I have known them all already, known them
    all:—
Have known the evenings, mornings, afternoons,
I have measured out my life with coffee spoons;
I know the voices dying with a dying fall
Beneath the music from a farther room.
  So how should I presume?

And I have known the eyes already, known them
    all—

The eyes that fix you in a formulated phrase,
And when I am formulated, sprawling on a pin,
When I am pinned and wriggling on the wall,
Then how should I begin
To spit out all the butt-ends of my days and ways?
  And how should I presume?

And I have known the arms already, known them
    all—
Arms that are braceleted and white and bare
[But in the lamplight, downed with light brown
    hair!]
Is it perfume from a dress
That makes me so digress?
Arms that lie along a table, or wrap about a shawl.
  And should I then presume?
  And how should I begin?

⋅　⋅　⋅　⋅　⋅

Shall I say, I have gone at dusk through narrow
    streets
And watched the smoke that rises from the pipes
Of lonely men in shirt-sleeves, leaning out of
    windows? . . .

I should have been a pair of ragged claws
Scuttling across the floors of silent seas.

⋅　⋅　⋅　⋅　⋅

And the afternoon, the evening, sleeps so peace-
    fully!
Smoothed by long fingers,
Asleep . . . tired . . . or it malingers,
Stretched on the floor, here beside you and me.
Should I, after tea and cakes and ices,
Have the strength to force the moment to its crisis?
But though I have wept and fasted, wept and prayed,
Though I have seen my head [grown slightly bald]
    brought in upon a platter,
I am no prophet—and here's no great matter;
I have seen the moment of my greatness flicker,
And I have seen the eternal Footman hold my coat,
    and snicker,
And in short, I was afraid.

And would it have been worth it, after all,
After the cups, the marmalade, the tea,
Among the porcelain, among some talk of you and
    me,
Would it have been worth while,
To have bitten off the matter with a smile,
To have squeezed the universe into a ball
To roll it toward some overwhelming question,
To say: "I am Lazarus, come from the dead,
Come back to tell you all, I shall tell you all"—

If one, settling a pillow by her head,
Should say: "That is not what I meant at all.
That is not it, at all."

And would it have been worth it, after all,
Would it have been worth while,
After the sunsets and the dooryards and the sprin-
kled streets,
After the novels, after the teacups, after the skirts
that trail along the floor—
And this, and so much more?—
It is impossible to say just what I mean!
But as if a magic lantern threw the nerves in patterns
on a screen:
Would it have been worth while
If one, settling a pillow or throwing off a shawl,
And turning toward the window, should say:
"That is not it at all,
That is not what I meant, at all."

.   .   .   .   .

No! I am not Prince Hamlet, nor was meant to be;
Am an attendant lord, one that will do
To swell a progress, start a scene or two,
Advise the prince; no doubt, an easy tool,
Deferential, glad to be of use,
Politic, cautious, and meticulous;

16

Full of high sentence, but a bit obtuse;
At times, indeed, almost ridiculous—
Almost, at times, the Fool.

I grow old . . . I grow old . . .
I shall wear the bottoms of my trousers rolled.

Shall I part my hair behind? Do I dare to eat a
    peach?
I shall wear white flannel trousers, and walk upon
    the beach.
I have heard the mermaids singing, each to each.

I do not think that they will sing to me.

I have seen them riding seaward on the waves
Combing the white hair of the waves blown back
When the wind blows the water white and black.

We have lingered in the chambers of the sea
By sea-girls wreathed with seaweed red and brown
Till human voices wake us, and we drown.

PORTRAIT OF A LADY

Thou hast committed—
Fornication: but that was in another country,
And besides, the wench is dead.
                    THE JEW OF MALTA.

I

AMONG the smoke and fog of a December afternoon
You have the scene arrange itself—as it will seem
    to do—
With "I have saved this afternoon for you";
And four wax candles in the darkened room,
Four rings of light upon the ceiling overhead,
An atmosphere of Juliet's tomb
Prepared for all the things to be said, or left unsaid.
We have been, let us say, to hear the latest Pole
Transmit the Preludes, through his hair and finger-
    tips.
"So intimate, this Chopin, that I think his soul
Should be resurrected only among friends
Some two or three, who will not touch the bloom
That is rubbed and questioned in the concert room."
—And so the conversation slips
Among velleities and carefully caught regrets
Through attenuated tones of violins
Mingled with remote cornets
And begins.

"You do not know how much they mean to me,
    my friends,
And how, how rare and strange it is, to find
In a life composed so much, so much of odds and
    ends,
[For indeed I do not love it . . . you knew? you
    are not blind!
How keen you are!]
To find a friend who has these qualities,
Who has, and gives
Those qualities upon which friendship lives.
How much it means that I say this to you—
Without these friendships—life, what *cauchemar!*"

Among the windings of the violins
And the ariettes
Of cracked cornets
Inside my brain a dull tom-tom begins
Absurdly hammering a prelude of its own,
Capricious monotone
That is at least one definite "false note."
—Let us take the air, in a tobacco trance,
Admire the monuments,
Discuss the late events,
Correct our watches by the public clocks.
Then sit for half an hour and drink our bocks.

II

Now that lilacs are in bloom
She has a bowl of lilacs in her room
And twists one in her fingers while she talks.
"Ah, my friend, you do not know, you do not
    know
What life is, you who hold it in your hands";
(Slowly twisting the lilac stalks)
"You let it flow from you, you let it flow,
And youth is cruel, and has no remorse
And smiles at situations which it cannot see."
I smile, of course,
And go on drinking tea.
"Yet with these April sunsets, that somehow recall
My buried life, and Paris in the Spring,
I feel immeasurably at peace, and find the world
To be wonderful and youthful, after all."

The voice returns like the insistent out-of-tune
Of a broken violin on an August afternoon:
"I am always sure that you understand
My feelings, always sure that you feel,
Sure that across the gulf you reach your hand.

You are invulnerable, you have no Achilles' heel.
You will go on, and when you have prevailed
You can say: at this point many a one has failed.

But what have I, but what have I, my friend,
To give you, what can you receive from me?
Only the friendship and the sympathy
Of one about to reach her journey's end.

I shall sit here, serving tea to friends. . . ."

I take my hat: how can I make a cowardly amends
For what she has said to me?
You will see me any morning in the park
Reading the comics and the sporting page.
Particularly I remark
An English countess goes upon the stage.
A Greek was murdered at a Polish dance,
Another bank defaulter has confessed.
I keep my countenance,
I remain self-possessed
Except when a street piano, mechanical and tired
Reiterates some worn-out common song
With the smell of hyacinths across the garden
Recalling things that other people have desired.
Are these ideas right or wrong?

III

The October night comes down; returning as before
Except for a slight sensation of being ill at ease
I mount the stairs and turn the handle of the door
And feel as if I had mounted on my hands and knees.

"And so you are going abroad; and when do you
      return?
But that's a useless question.
You hardly know when you are coming back,
You will find so much to learn."
My smile falls heavily among the bric-à-brac.

"Perhaps you can write to me."
My self-possession flares up for a second;
This is as I had reckoned.
"I have been wondering frequently of late
(But our beginnings never know our ends!)
Why we have not developed into friends."
I feel like one who smiles, and turning shall remark
Suddenly, his expression in a glass.
My self-possession gutters; we are really in the dark.

"For everybody said so, all our friends,
They all were sure our feelings would relate
So closely! I myself can hardly understand.
We must leave it now to fate.
You will write, at any rate.
Perhaps it is not too late.
I shall sit here, serving tea to friends."

And I must borrow every changing shape
To find expression . . . dance, dance
Like a dancing bear,

Cry like a parrot, chatter like an ape.
Let us take the air, in a tobacco trance—

Well! and what if she should die some afternoon,
Afternoon grey and smoky, evening yellow and
    rose;
Should die and leave me sitting pen in hand
With the smoke coming down above the housetops;
Doubtful, for a while
Not knowing what to feel or if I understand
Or whether wise or foolish, tardy or too soon . . .
Would she not have the advantage, after all?
This music is successful with a "dying fall"
Now that we talk of dying—
And should I have the right to smile?

PRELUDES

I

THE winter evening settles down
With smell of steaks in passageways.
Six o'clock.
The burnt-out ends of smoky days.
And now a gusty shower wraps
The grimy scraps
Of withered leaves about your feet
And newspapers from vacant lots;
The showers beat
On broken blinds and chimney-pots,
And at the corner of the street
A lonely cab-horse steams and stamps.
And then the lighting of the lamps.

II

The morning comes to consciousness
Of faint stale smells of beer
From the sawdust-trampled street
With all its muddy feet that press
To early coffee-stands.
With the other masquerades
That time resumes,
One thinks of all the hands
That are raising dingy shades
In a thousand furnished rooms.

III

You tossed a blanket from the bed,
You lay upon your back, and waited;
You dozed, and watched the night revealing
The thousand sordid images
Of which your soul was constituted;
They flickered against the ceiling.
And when all the world came back
And the light crept up between the shutters
And you heard the sparrows in the gutters,
You had such a vision of the street
As the street hardly understands;
Sitting along the bed's edge, where
You curled the papers from your hair,
Or clasped the yellow soles of feet
In the palms of both soiled hands.

IV

His soul stretched tight across the skies
That fade behind a city block,
Or trampled by insistent feet
At four and five and six o'clock;
And short square fingers stuffing pipes,
And evening newspapers, and eyes
Assured of certain certainties,
The conscience of a blackened street
Impatient to assume the world.

I am moved by fancies that are curled
Around these images, and cling:
The notion of some infinitely gentle
Infinitely suffering thing.

Wipe your hand across your mouth, and laugh;
The worlds revolve like ancient women
Gathering fuel in vacant lots.

RHAPSODY ON A WINDY NIGHT

TWELVE o'clock.
Along the reaches of the street
Held in a lunar synthesis,
Whispering lunar incantations
Dissolve the floors of memory
And all its clear relations
Its divisions and precisions,
Every street lamp that I pass
Beats like a fatalistic drum,
And through the spaces of the dark
Midnight shakes the memory
As a madman shakes a dead geranium.

Half-past one,
The street-lamp sputtered,
The street-lamp muttered,
The street-lamp said, "Regard that woman
Who hesitates toward you in the light of the door
Which opens on her like a grin.
You see the border of her dress
Is torn and stained with sand,
And you see the corner of her eye
Twists like a crooked pin."

The memory throws up high and dry
A crowd of twisted things;

A twisted branch upon the beach
Eaten smooth, and polished
As if the world gave up
The secret of its skeleton,
Stiff and white.
A broken spring in a factory yard,
Rust that clings to the form that the strength has left
Hard and curled and ready to snap.

Half-past two,
The street-lamp said,
"Remark the cat which flattens itself in the gutter,
Slips out its tongue
And devours a morsel of rancid butter."
So the hand of the child, automatic,
Slipped out and pocketed a toy that was running
    along the quay.
I could see nothing behind that child's eye.
I have seen eyes in the street
Trying to peer through lighted shutters,
And a crab one afternoon in a pool,
An old crab with barnacles on his back,
Gripped the end of a stick which I held him.

Half-past three,
The lamp sputtered,
The lamp muttered in the dark.

The lamp hummed:
"Regard the moon,
La lune ne garde aucune rancune,
She winks a feeble eye,
She smiles into corners.
She smooths the hair of the grass.
The moon has lost her memory.
A washed-out smallpox cracks her face,
Her hand twists a paper rose,
That smells of dust and eau de Cologne,
She is alone
With all the old nocturnal smells
That cross and cross across her brain."
The reminiscence comes
Of sunless dry geraniums
And dust in crevices,
Smells of chestnuts in the streets,
And female smells in shuttered rooms,
And cigarettes in corridors
And cocktail smells in bars.

The lamp said,
"Four o'clock,
Here is the number on the door.
Memory!
You have the key,

The little lamp spreads a ring on the stair.
Mount.
The bed is open; the tooth-brush hangs on the wall,
Put your shoes at the door, sleep, prepare for life."

The last twist of the knife.

MORNING AT THE WINDOW

THEY are rattling breakfast plates in basement
    kitchens,
And along the trampled edges of the street
I am aware of the damp souls of housemaids
Sprouting despondently at area gates.

The brown waves of fog toss up to me
Twisted faces from the bottom of the street,
And tear from a passer-by with muddy skirts
An aimless smile that hovers in the air
And vanishes along the level of the roofs.

THE *BOSTON EVENING TRANSCRIPT*

THE readers of the *Boston Evening Transcript*
Sway in the wind like a field of ripe corn.

When evening quickens faintly in the street,
Wakening the appetites of life in some
And to others bringing the *Boston Evening Tran-
script,*
I mount the steps and ring the bell, turning
Wearily, as one would turn to nod good-bye to
Rochefoucauld,
If the street were time and he at the end of the street,
And I say, "Cousin Harriet, here is the *Boston
Evening Transcript.*"

AUNT HELEN

Miss Helen Slingsby was my maiden aunt,
And lived in a small house near a fashionable square
Cared for by servants to the number of four.
Now when she died there was silence in heaven
And silence at her end of the street.
The shutters were drawn and the undertaker wiped
    his feet—
He was aware that this sort of thing had occurred
    before.
The dogs were handsomely provided for,
But shortly afterwards the parrot died too.
The Dresden clock continued ticking on the mantel-
    piece,
And the footman sat upon the dining-table
Holding the second housemaid on his knees—
Who had always been so careful while her mistress
    lived.

COUSIN NANCY

Miss Nancy Ellicott
Strode across the hills and broke them,
Rode across the hills and broke them—
The barren New England hills—
Riding to hounds
Over the cow-pasture.

Miss Nancy Ellicott smoked
And danced all the modern dances;
And her aunts were not quite sure how they felt
    about it,
But they knew that it was modern.

Upon the glazen shelves kept watch
Matthew and Waldo, guardians of the faith,
The army of unalterable law.

MR. APOLLINAX

Ω τῆς καινότητος. Ἡράκλεις, τῆς παραδοξολογίας.
εὐμήχανος ἄνθρωπος.

LUCIAN.

WHEN Mr. Apollinax visited the United States
His laughter tinkled among the teacups.
I thought of Fragilion, that shy figure among the
    birch-trees,
And of Priapus in the shrubbery
Gaping at the lady in the swing.
In the palace of Mrs. Phlaccus, at Professor Chan-
    ning-Cheetah's
He laughed like an irresponsible fœtus.
His laughter was submarine and profound
Like the old man of the sea's
Hidden under coral islands
Where worried bodies of drowned men drift down
    in the green silence,
Dropping from fingers of surf.
I looked for the head of Mr. Apollinax rolling under
    a chair

Or grinning over a screen
With seaweed in its hair.
I heard the beat of centaur's hoofs over the hard turf
As his dry and passionate talk devoured the after-
    noon.

35

"He is a charming man"—"But after all what did
    he mean?"—
"His pointed ears. . . . He must be unbalanced,"—
"There was something he said that I might have
    challenged."
Of dowager Mrs. Phlaccus, and Professor and Mrs.
    Cheetah
I remember a slice of lemon, and a bitten macaroon.

HYSTERIA

As she laughed I was aware of becoming involved in her laughter and being part of it, until her teeth were only accidental stars with a talent for squad-drill. I was drawn in by short gasps, inhaled at each momentary recovery, lost finally in the dark caverns of her throat, bruised by the ripple of unseen muscles. An elderly waiter with trembling hands was hurriedly spreading a pink and white checked cloth over the rusty green iron table, saying: "If the lady and gentleman wish to take their tea in the garden, if the lady and gentleman wish to take their tea in the garden . . ." I decided that if the shaking of her breasts could be stopped, some of the fragments of the afternoon might be collected, and I concentrated my attention with careful subtlety to this end.

CONVERSATION GALANTE

I OBSERVE: "Our sentimental friend the moon!
Or possibly (fantastic, I confess)
It may be Prester John's balloon
Or an old battered lantern hung aloft
To light poor travellers to their distress."
   She then: "How you digress!"

And I then: "Someone frames upon the keys
That exquisite nocturne, with which we explain
The night and moonshine; music which we seize
To body forth our own vacuity."
   She then: "Does this refer to me?"
   "Oh no, it is I who am inane."

"You, madam, are the eternal humorist,
The eternal enemy of the absolute,
Giving our vagrant moods the slightest twist!
With your air indifferent and imperious
At a stroke our mad poetics to confute—"
   And—"Are we then so serious?"

LA FIGLIA CHE PIANGE

O quam te memorem virgo . . .

STAND on the highest pavement of the stair—
Lean on a garden urn—
Weave, weave the sunlight in your hair—
Clasp your flowers to you with a pained surprise—
Fling them to the ground and turn
With a fugitive resentment in your eyes:
But weave, weave the sunlight in your hair.

So I would have had him leave,
So I would have had her stand and grieve,
So he would have left
As the soul leaves the body torn and bruised,
As the mind deserts the body it has used.
I should find
Some way incomparably light and deft,
Some way we both should understand,
Simple and faithless as a smile and shake of the hand.

She turned away, but with the autumn weather
Compelled my imagination many days,
Many days and many hours:
Her hair over her arms and her arms full of flowers.
And I wonder how they should have been together!
I should have lost a gesture and a pose.
Sometimes these cogitations still amaze
The troubled midnight and the noon's repose.

POEMS

1920

GERONTION

Thou hast nor youth nor age
But as it were an after dinner sleep
Dreaming of both.

HERE I am, an old man in a dry month,
Being read to by a boy, waiting for rain.
I was neither at the hot gates
Nor fought in the warm rain
Nor knee deep in the salt marsh, heaving a cutlass,
Bitten by flies, fought.
My house is a decayed house,
And the jew squats on the window sill, the owner,
Spawned in some estaminet of Antwerp,
Blistered in Brussels, patched and peeled in London.
The goat coughs at night in the field overhead;
Rocks, moss, stonecrop, iron, merds.
The woman keeps the kitchen, makes tea,
Sneezes at evening, poking the peevish gutter.
                              I an old man,
A dull head among windy spaces.

Signs are taken for wonders. "We would see a
    sign!"
The word within a word, unable to speak a word,
Swaddled with darkness. In the juvescence of the
    year
Came Christ the tiger

In depraved May, dogwood and chestnut, flowering
  judas,
To be eaten, to be divided, to be drunk
Among whispers; by Mr. Silvero
With caressing hands, at Limoges
Who walked all night in the next room;

By Hakagawa, bowing among the Titians;
By Madame de Tornquist, in the dark room
Shifting the candles; Fräulein von Kulp
Who turned in the hall, one hand on the door.
  Vacant shuttles
Weave the wind. I have no ghosts,
An old man in a draughty house
Under a windy knob.

After such knowledge, what forgiveness? Think
  now
History has many cunning passages, contrived
  corridors
And issues, deceives with whispering ambitions,
Guides us by vanities. Think now
She gives when our attention is distracted
And what she gives, gives with such supple confu-
  sions
That the giving famishes the craving. Gives too
  late

What's not believed in, or if still believed,
In memory only, reconsidered passion. Gives too
      soon
Into weak hands, what's thought can be dispensed
      with
Till the refusal propagates a fear. Think
Neither fear nor courage saves us. Unnatural vices
Are fathered by our heroism. Virtues
Are forced upon us by our impudent crimes.
These tears are shaken from the wrath-bearing tree.

The tiger springs in the new year. Us he devours.
      Think at last
We have not reached conclusion, when I
Stiffen in a rented house. Think at last
I have not made this show purposelessly
And it is not by any concitation
Of the backward devils
I would meet you upon this honestly.
I that was near your heart was removed there-
      from
To lose beauty in terror, terror in inquisition.
I have lost my passion: why should I need to keep it
Since what is kept must be adulterated?
I have lost my sight, smell, hearing, taste and touch:
How should I use them for your closer contact?

These with a thousand small deliberations
Protract the profit of their chilled delirium,
Excite the membrane, when the sense has cooled,
With pungent sauces, multiply variety
In a wilderness of mirrors. What will the spider do,
Suspend its operations, will the weevil
Delay? De Bailhache, Fresca, Mrs. Cammel,
        whirled
Beyond the circuit of the shuddering Bear
In fractured atoms. Gull against the wind, in the
        windy straits
Of Belle Isle, or running on the Horn,
White feathers in the snow, the Gulf claims,
And an old man driven by the Trades
To a sleepy corner.

                        Tenants of the house,
Thoughts of a dry brain in a dry season.

BURBANK WITH A BAEDEKER: BLEISTEIN WITH A CIGAR

Tra-la-la-la-la-la-laire—nil nisi divinum stabile est; cae-
tera fumus—the gondola stopped, the old palace was there,
how charming its grey and pink—goats and monkeys, with
such hair too!—so the countess passed on until she came through
the little park, where Niobe presented her with a cabinet, and
so departed.

BURBANK crossed a little bridge
  Descending at a small hotel;
Princess Volupine arrived,
  They were together, and he fell.

Defunctive music under sea
  Passed seaward with the passing bell
Slowly: the God Hercules
  Had left him, that had loved him well.

The horses, under the axletree
  Beat up the dawn from Istria
With even feet. Her shuttered barge
  Burned on the water all the day.

But this or such was Bleistein's way:
  A saggy bending of the knees
And elbows, with the palms turned out,
  Chicago Semite Viennese.

A lustreless protrusive eye
  Stares from the protozoic slime
At a perspective of Canaletto.
  The smoky candle end of time

Declines. On the Rialto once.
  The rats are underneath the piles.
The jew is underneath the lot.
  Money in furs. The boatman smiles,

Princess Volupine extends
  A meagre, blue-nailed, phthisic hand
To climb the waterstair. Lights, lights,
  She entertains Sir Ferdinand

Klein. Who clipped the lion's wings
  And flea'd his rump and pared his claws?
Thought Burbank, meditating on
  Time's ruins, and the seven laws.

SWEENEY ERECT

And the trees about me,
Let them be dry and leafless; let the rocks
Groan with continual surges; and behind me
Make all a desolation. Look, look, wenches!

PAINT me a cavernous waste shore
    Cast in the unstilled Cyclades,
Paint me the bold anfractuous rocks
    Faced by the snarled and yelping seas.

Display me Aeolus above
    Reviewing the insurgent gales
Which tangle Ariadne's hair
    And swell with haste the perjured sails.

Morning stirs the feet and hands
    (Nausicaa and Polypheme).
Gesture of orang-outang
    Rises from the sheets in steam.

This withered root of knots of hair
    Slitted below and gashed with eyes,
This oval O cropped out with teeth:
    The sickle motion from the thighs

Jackknifes upward at the knees
    Then straightens out from heel to hip

Pushing the framework of the bed
  And clawing at the pillow slip.

Sweeney addressed full length to shave
  Broadbottomed, pink from nape to base,
Knows the female temperament
  And wipes the suds around his face.

(The lengthened shadow of a man
  Is history, said Emerson
Who had not seen the silhouette
  Of Sweeney straddled in the sun.)

Tests the razor on his leg
  Waiting until the shriek subsides.
The epileptic on the bed
  Curves backward, clutching at her sides.

The ladies of the corridor
  Find themselves involved, disgraced,
Call witness to their principles
  And deprecate the lack of taste

Observing that hysteria
  Might easily be misunderstood;
Mrs. Turner intimates
  It does the house no sort of good.

But Doris, towelled from the bath,
    Enters padding on broad feet,
Bringing sal volatile
    And a glass of brandy neat.

A COOKING EGG

En l'an trentiesme de mon aage
Que toutes mes hontes j'ay beues . . .

PIPIT sate upright in her chair
   Some distance from where I was sitting;
Views of the Oxford Colleges
   Lay on the table, with the knitting.

Daguerreotypes and silhouettes,
   Her grandfather and great great aunts,
Supported on the mantelpiece
   An *Invitation to the Dance*.

   .   .   .   .   .

I shall not want Honour in Heaven
   For I shall meet Sir Philip Sidney
And have talk with Coriolanus
   And other heroes of that kidney.

I shall not want Capital in Heaven
   For I shall meet Sir Alfred Mond.
We two shall lie together, lapt
   In a five per cent. Exchequer Bond.

I shall not want Society in Heaven,
   Lucretia Borgia shall be my Bride;

Her anecdotes will be more amusing
    Than Pipit's experience could provide.

I shall not want Pipit in Heaven:
    Madame Blavatsky will instruct me
In the Seven Sacred Trances;
    Piccarda de Donati will conduct me.

    .   .   .   .   .

But where is the penny world I bought
    To eat with Pipit behind the screen?
The red-eyed scavengers are creeping
    From Kentish Town and Golder's Green;

Where are the eagles and the trumpets?

    Buried beneath some snow-deep Alps.
Over buttered scones and crumpets
    Weeping, weeping multitudes
Droop in a hundred A.B.C.'s

LE DIRECTEUR

MALHEUR à la malheureuse Tamise
Qui coule si près du Spectateur.
Le directeur
Conservateur
Du Spectateur
Empeste la brise.
Les actionnaires
Réactionnaires
Du Spectateur
Conservateur
Bras dessus bras dessous
Font des tours
A pas de loup.
Dans un égout
Une petite fille
En guenilles
Camarde
Regarde
Le directeur
Du Spectateur
Conservateur
Et crève d'amour.

En Amerique, professeur;
En Angleterre, journaliste;
C'est à grands pas et en sueur
Que vous suivrez à peine ma piste.
En Yorkshire, conférencier;
A Londres, un peu banquier,
Vous me paierez bien la tête.
C'est à Paris que je me coiffe
Casque noir de jemenfoutiste.
En Allemagne, philosophe
Surexcité par Emporheben
Au grand air de Bergsteigleben;
J'erre toujours de-ci de-là
A divers coups de tra là là
De Damas jusqu'à Omaha.
Je célébrai mon jour de fête
Dans une oasis d'Afrique
Vetu d'une peau de girafe.

On montrera mon cénotaphe
Aux côtes brulantes de Mozambique.

LUNE DE MIEL

Ils ont vu les Pays-Bas, ils rentrent à Terre Haute;
Mais une nuit d'été, les voici à Ravenne,
A l'aise entre deux draps, chez deux centaines de
    punaises;
La sueur aestivale, et une forte odeur de chienne.
Ils restent sur le dos écartant les genoux
De quatre jambes molles tout gonflées de morsures.
On relève le drap pour mieux égratigner.
Moins d'une lieue d'ici est Saint Apollinaire]
En Classe, basilique connue des amateurs
De chapitaux d'acanthe que tournoie le vent.

Ils vont prendre le train de huit heures
Prolonger leurs misères de Padoue à Milan
Où se trouvent la Cène, et un restaurant pas cher.
Lui pense aux pourboires, et rédige son bilan.
Ils auront vu la Suisse et traversé la France.
Et Saint Apollinaire, raide et ascétique,
Vieille usine désaffectée de Dieu, tient encore
Dans ses pierres écroulantes la forme précise de
    Byzance.

THE HIPPOPOTAMUS

*Similiter et omnes revereantur Diaconos, ut mandatum Jesu
Christi; et Episcopum, ut Jesum Christum, existentem filium
Patris; Presbyteros autem, ut concilium Dei et conjunctionem
Apostolorum. Sine his Ecclesia non vocatur; de quibus suadeo
vos sic habeo.* S. IGNATII AD TRALLIANOS.

*And when this epistle is read among you, cause that it be
read also in the church of the Laodiceans.*

THE broad-backed hippopotamus
Rests on his belly in the mud;
Although he seems so firm to us
He is merely flesh and blood.

Flesh and blood is weak and frail,
Susceptible to nervous shock;
While the True Church can never fail
For it is based upon a rock.

The hippo's feeble steps may err
In compassing material ends,
While the True Church need never stir
To gather in its dividends.

The 'potamus can never reach
The mango on the mango-tree;
But fruits of pomegranate and peach
Refresh the Church from over sea.

At mating time the hippo's voice
Betrays inflexions hoarse and odd,
But every week we hear rejoice
The Church, at being one with God.

The hippopotamus's day
Is passed in sleep; at night he hunts;
God works in a mysterious way—
The Church can sleep and feed at once.

I saw the 'potamus take wing
Ascending from the damp savannas,
And quiring angels round him sing
The praise of God, in loud hosannas.

Blood of the Lamb shall wash him clean
And him shall heavenly arms enfold,
Among the saints he shall be seen
Performing on a harp of gold.

He shall be washed as white as snow,
By all the martyr'd virgins kist,
While the True Church remains below
Wrapt in the old miasmal mist.

DANS LE RESTAURANT

LE garçon délabré qui n'a rien à faire
Que de se gratter les doigts et se pencher sur mon
    épaule:
  "Dans mon pays il fera temps pluvieux,
  Du vent, du grand soleil, et de la pluie;
  C'est ce qu'on appelle le jour de lessive des gueux."
(Bavard, baveux, à la croupe arrondie,
Je te prie, au moins, ne bave pas dans la soupe).
  "Les saules trempés, et des bourgeons sur les
    ronces—
  C'est là, dans une averse, qu'on s'abrite.
J'avais sept ans, elle était plus petite.
  Elle était toute mouillée, je lui ai donné des
    primevères."
Les taches de son gilet montent au chiffre de trente-
    huit.
  "Je la chatouillais, pour la faire rire.
  J'éprouvais un instant de puissance et de délire."

  Mais alors, vieux lubrique, à cet âge . . .
"Monsieur, le fait est dur.
  Il est venu, nous peloter, un gros chien;
  Moi j'avais peur, je l'ai quittée à mi-chemin.
  C'est dommage."
    Mais alors, tu as ton vautour!

Va t'en te décrotter les rides du visage;
Tiens, ma fourchette, décrasse-toi le crâne.
De quel droit payes-tu des expériences comme moi?
Tiens, voilà dix sous, pour la salle-de-bains.

Phlébas, le Phénicien, pendant quinze jours noyé,
Oubliait les cris des mouettes et la houle de Cornou-
    aille,
Et les profits et les pertes, et la cargaison d'étain:
Un courant de sous-mer l'emporta très loin,
Le repassant aux étapes de sa vie antérieure.
Figurez-vous donc, c'était un sort pénible;
Cependant, ce fut jadis un bel homme, de haute
    taille.

WHISPERS OF IMMORTALITY

WEBSTER was much possessed by death
And saw the skull beneath the skin;
And breastless creatures under ground
Leaned backward with a lipless grin.

Daffodil bulbs instead of balls
Stared from the sockets of the eyes!
He knew that thought clings round dead limbs
Tightening its lusts and luxuries.

Donne, I suppose, was such another
Who found no substitute for sense,
To seize and clutch and penetrate;
Expert beyond experience,

He knew the anguish of the marrow
The ague of the skeleton;
No contact possible to flesh
Allayed the fever of the bone.

.   .   .   .   .

Grishkin is nice: her Russian eye
Is underlined for emphasis;
Uncorseted, her friendly bust
Gives promise of pneumatic bliss.

The couched Brazilian jaguar
Compels the scampering marmoset
With subtle effluence of cat;
Grishkin has a maisonette;

The sleek Brazilian jaguar
Does not in its arboreal gloom
Distil so rank a feline smell
As Grishkin in a drawing-room.

And even the Abstract Entities
Circumambulate her charm;
But our lot crawls between dry ribs
To keep our metaphysics warm.

MR. ELIOT'S
SUNDAY MORNING SERVICE

Look, look, master, here comes two religious caterpillars.
THE JEW OF MALTA.

POLYPHILOPROGENITIVE
The sapient sutlers of the Lord
Drift across the window-panes.
In the beginning was the Word.

In the beginning was the Word.
Superfetation of τὸ ἕν,
And at the mensual turn of time
Produced enervate Origen.

A painter of the Umbrian school
Designed upon a gesso ground
The nimbus of the Baptized God.
The wilderness is cracked and browned

But through the water pale and thin
Still shine the unoffending feet
And there above the painter set
The Father and the Paraclete.
.   .   .   .   .

The sable presbyters approach
The avenue of penitence;

The young are red and pustular
Clutching piaculative pence.

Under the penitential gates
Sustained by staring Seraphim
Where the souls of the devout
Burn invisible and dim.

Along the garden-wall the bees
With hairy bellies pass between
The staminate and pistilate,
Blest office of the epicene.

Sweeney shifts from ham to ham
Stirring the water in his bath.
The masters of the subtle schools
Are controversial, polymath.

SWEENEY
AMONG THE NIGHTINGALES

ὤμοι, πέπληγμαι καιρίαν πληγὴν ἔσω.

APENECK SWEENEY spreads his knees
Letting his arms hang down to laugh,
The zebra stripes along his jaw
Swelling to maculate giraffe.

The circles of the stormy moon
Slide westward toward the River Plate,
Death and the Raven drift above
And Sweeney guards the hornèd gate.

Gloomy Orion and the Dog
Are veiled; and hushed the shrunken seas;
The person in the Spanish cape
Tries to sit on Sweeney's knees

Slips and pulls the table cloth
Overturns a coffee-cup,
Reorganised upon the floor
She yawns and draws a stocking up;

The silent man in mocha brown
Sprawls at the window-sill and gapes;
The waiter brings in oranges
Bananas figs and hothouse grapes;

The silent vertebrate in brown
Contracts and concentrates, withdraws;
Rachel *née* Rabinovitch
Tears at the grapes with murderous paws;

She and the lady in the cape
Are suspect, thought to be in league;
Therefore the man with heavy eyes
Declines the gambit, shows fatigue,

Leaves the room and reappears
Outside the window, leaning in,
Branches of wistaria
Circumscribe a golden grin;

The host with someone indistinct
Converses at the door apart,
The nightingales are singing near
The Convent of the Sacred Heart,

And sang within the bloody wood
When Agamemnon cried aloud,
And let their liquid siftings fall
To stain the stiff dishonoured shroud.

THE WASTE LAND
1922

"NAM Sibyllam quidem Cumis ego ipse oculis meis vidi in ampulla pendere, et cum illi pueri dicerent: Σίβυλλα τί θέλεις; respondebat illa: ἀποθανεῖν θέλω."

For Ezra Pound
il miglior fabbro.

I. THE BURIAL OF THE DEAD

APRIL is the cruellest month, breeding
Lilacs out of the dead land, mixing
Memory and desire, stirring
Dull roots with spring rain.
Winter kept us warm, covering
Earth in forgetful snow, feeding
A little life with dried tubers.
Summer surprised us, coming over the Starnber-
  gersee
With a shower of rain; we stopped in the colonnade,
And went on in sunlight, into the Hofgarten,   10
And drank coffee, and talked for an hour.
Bin gar keine Russin, stamm' aus Litauen, echt
  deutsch.
And when we were children, staying at the arch-
  duke's,
My cousin's, he took me out on a sled,
And I was frightened. He said, Marie,
Marie, hold on tight. And down we went.
In the mountains, there you feel free.
I read, much of the night, and go south in the winter.

What are the roots that clutch, what branches grow
Out of this stony rubbish? Son of man,   20
You cannot say, or guess, for you know only
A heap of broken images, where the sun beats,

And the dead tree gives no shelter, the cricket no
    relief,
And the dry stone no sound of water. Only
There is shadow under this red rock,
(Come in under the shadow of this red rock),
And I will show you something different from either
Your shadow at morning striding behind you
Or your shadow at evening rising to meet you;
I will show you fear in a handful of dust.   30

        Frisch weht der Wind
        Der Heimat zu
        Mein Irisch Kind,
        Wo weilest du?

"You gave me hyacinths first a year ago;
"They called me the hyacinth girl."
—Yet when we came back, late, from the Hyacinth
    garden,
Your arms full, and your hair wet, I could not
Speak, and my eyes failed, I was neither
Living nor dead, and I knew nothing,   40
Looking into the heart of light, the silence.
Oed' und leer das Meer.

Madame Sosostris, famous clairvoyante,
Had a bad cold, nevertheless
Is known to be the wisest woman in Europe,

With a wicked pack of cards. Here, said she,
Is your card, the drowned Phoenician Sailor,
(Those are pearls that were his eyes. Look!)
Here is Belladonna, the Lady of the Rocks,
The lady of situations.   50
Here is the man with three staves, and here the
        Wheel,
And here is the one-eyed merchant, and this card,
Which is blank, is something he carries on his back,
Which I am forbidden to see. I do not find
The Hanged Man. Fear death by water.
I see crowds of people, walking round in a ring.
Thank you. If you see dear Mrs. Equitone,
Tell her I bring the horoscope myself:
One must be so careful these days.

Unreal City,   60
Under the brown fog of a winter dawn,
A crowd flowed over London Bridge, so many,
I had not thought death had undone so many.
Sighs, short and infrequent, were exhaled,
And each man fixed his eyes before his feet.
Flowed up the hill and down King William Street,
To where Saint Mary Woolnoth kept the hours
With a dead sound on the final stroke of nine.
There I saw one I knew, and stopped him, crying:
        "Stetson!

"You who were with me in the ships at Mylae! 70
"That corpse you planted last year in your garden,
"Has it begun to sprout? Will it bloom this year?
"Or has the sudden frost disturbed its bed?
"Oh keep the Dog far hence, that's friend to men,
"Or with his nails he'll dig it up again!
"You! hypocrite lecteur!—mon semblable,—mon frère!"

II. A GAME OF CHESS

THE Chair she sat in, like a burnished throne,
Glowed on the marble, where the glass
Held up by standards wrought with fruited vines
From which a golden Cupidon peeped out   80
(Another hid his eyes behind his wing)
Doubled the flames of sevenbranched candelabra
Reflecting light upon the table as
The glitter of her jewels rose to meet it,
From satin cases poured in rich profusion;
In vials of ivory and coloured glass
Unstoppered, lurked her strange synthetic perfumes,
Unguent, powdered, or liquid—troubled, confused
And drowned the sense in odours; stirred by the air
That freshened from the window, these ascended
In fattening the prolonged candle-flames,   91
Flung their smoke into the laquearia,
Stirring the pattern on the coffered ceiling.
Huge sea-wood fed with copper
Burned green and orange, framed by the coloured
        stone,
In which sad light a carvèd dolphin swam.
Above the antique mantel was displayed
As though a window gave upon the sylvan scene
The change of Philomel, by the barbarous king

So rudely forced; yet there the nightingale 100
Filled all the desert with inviolable voice
And still she cried, and still the world pursues,
"Jug Jug" to dirty ears.
And other withered stumps of time
Were told upon the walls; staring forms
Leaned out, leaning, hushing the room enclosed.
Footsteps shuffled on the stair.
Under the firelight, under the brush, her hair
Spread out in fiery points
Glowed into words, then would be savagely still. 110

"My nerves are bad to-night. Yes, bad. Stay
    with me.
"Speak to me. Why do you never speak. Speak.
  "What are you thinking of? What thinking?
    What?
"I never know what you are thinking. Think."

I think we are in rats' alley
Where the dead men lost their bones.

"What is that noise?"
                    The wind under the door.
"What is that noise now? What is the wind doing?"
                    Nothing again nothing. 120

                              "Do
"You know nothing? Do you see nothing? Do
    you remember
"Nothing?"

    I remember
Those are pearls that were his eyes.
"Are you alive, or not? Is there nothing in your
    head?"
                                        But
O O O O that Shakespeherian Rag—
It's so elegant
So intelligent   130
"What shall I do now? What shall I do?"
"I shall rush out as I am, and walk the street
"With my hair down, so. What shall we do to-
    morrow?
"What shall we ever do?"
                          The hot water at ten.
And if it rains, a closed car at four.
And we shall play a game of chess,
Pressing lidless eyes and waiting for a knock upon
    the door.

When Lil's husband got demobbed, I said—
I didn't mince my words, I said to her myself, 140
HURRY UP PLEASE ITS TIME
                    75

Now Albert's coming back, make yourself a bit
    smart.
He'll want to know what you done with that money
    he gave you
To get yourself some teeth. He did, I was there.
You have them all out, Lil, and get a nice set,
He said, I swear, I can't bear to look at you.
And no more can't I, I said, and think of poor
    Albert,
He's been in the army four years, he wants a good
    time,
And if you don't give it him, there's others will, I
    said.
Oh is there, she said. Something o' that, I said. 150
Then I'll know who to thank, she said, and give
    me a straight look.
HURRY UP PLEASE ITS TIME
If you don't like it you can get on with it, I said.
Others can pick and choose if you can't.
But if Albert makes off, it won't be for lack of telling.
You ought to be ashamed, I said, to look so antique.
(And her only thirty-one.)
I can't help it, she said, pulling a long face,
It's them pills I took, to bring it off, she said.
(She's had five already, and nearly died of young
    George.)   160

The chemist said it would be all right, but I've never
been the same.

You *are* a proper fool, I said.

Well, if Albert won't leave you alone, there it is, I
said,

What you get married for if you don't want children?

HURRY UP PLEASE ITS TIME

Well, that Sunday Albert was home, they had a
hot gammon,

And they asked me in to dinner, to get the beauty
of it hot—

HURRY UP PLEASE ITS TIME

HURRY UP PLEASE ITS TIME

Goonight Bill. Goonight Lou. Goonight May.
Goonight.   170

Ta ta. Goonight. Goonight.

Good night, ladies, good night, sweet ladies, good
night, good night.

III. THE FIRE SERMON

THE river's tent is broken: the last fingers of leaf
Clutch and sink into the wet bank. The wind
Crosses the brown land, unheard. The nymphs are
    departed.
Sweet Thames, run softly, till I end my song.
The river bears no empty bottles, sandwich papers,
Silk handkerchiefs, cardboard boxes, cigarette ends
Or other testimony of summer nights. The nymphs
    are departed.
And their friends, the loitering heirs of city di-
    rectors;   180
Departed, have left no addresses.
By the waters of Leman I sat down and wept . . .
Sweet Thames, run softly till I end my song,
Sweet Thames, run softly, for I speak not loud or
    long.
But at my back in a cold blast I hear
The rattle of the bones, and chuckle spread from
    ear to ear.
A rat crept softly through the vegetation
Dragging its slimy belly on the bank
While I was fishing in the dull canal
On a winter evening round behind the gashouse 190
Musing upon the king my brother's wreck

78

And on the king my father's death before him.
White bodies naked on the low damp ground
And bones cast in a little low dry garret,
Rattled by the rat's foot only, year to year.
But at my back from time to time I hear
The sound of horns and motors, which shall bring
Sweeney to Mrs. Porter in the spring.
O the moon shone bright on Mrs. Porter
And on her daughter   200
They wash their feet in soda water
Et O ces voix d'enfants, chantant dans la coupole!

Twit twit twit
Jug jug jug jug jug jug
So rudely forc'd.
Tereu

Unreal City
Under the brown fog of a winter noon
Mr. Eugenides, the Smyrna merchant
Unshaven, with a pocket full of currants   210
C.i.f. London: documents at sight,
Asked me in demotic French
To luncheon at the Cannon Street Hotel
Followed by a weekend at the Metropole.

At the violet hour, when the eyes and back
Turn upward from the desk, when the human en-
    gine waits
Like a taxi throbbing waiting,
I Tiresias, though blind, throbbing between two
    lives,
Old man with wrinkled female breasts, can see
At the violet hour, the evening hour that strives 220
Homeward, and brings the sailor home from sea,
The typist home at teatime, clears her breakfast,
    lights
Her stove, and lays out food in tins.
Out of the window perilously spread
Her drying combinations touched by the sun's last
    rays,
On the divan are piled (at night her bed)
Stockings, slippers, camisoles, and stays.
I Tiresias, old man with wrinkled dugs
Perceived the scene, and foretold the rest—
I too awaited the expected guest.   230
He, the young man carbuncular, arrives,
A small house agent's clerk, with one bold stare,
One of the low on whom assurance sits
As a silk hat on a Bradford millionaire.
The time is now propitious, as he guesses,
The meal is ended, she is bored and tired,

Endeavours to engage her in caresses
Which still are unreproved, if undesired.
Flushed and decided, he assaults at once;
Exploring hands encounter no defence; 240
His vanity requires no response,
And makes a welcome of indifference.
(And I Tiresias have foresuffered all
Enacted on this same divan or bed;
I who have sat by Thebes below the wall
And walked among the lowest of the dead.)
Bestows one final patronising kiss,
And gropes his way, finding the stairs unlit . . .

She turns and looks a moment in the glass,
Hardly aware of her departed lover; 250
Her brain allows one half-formed thought to pass:
"Well now that's done: and I'm glad it's over."
When lovely woman stoops to folly and
Paces about her room again, alone,
She smoothes her hair with automatic hand,
And puts a record on the gramophone.

"This music crept by me upon the waters"
And along the Strand, up Queen Victoria Street.
O City city, I can sometimes hear
Beside a public bar in Lower Thames Street, 260

The pleasant whining of a mandoline
And a clatter and a chatter from within
Where fishmen lounge at noon: where the walls
Of Magnus Martyr hold
Inexplicable splendour of Ionian white and gold.

     The river sweats
     Oil and tar
     The barges drift
     With the turning tide
     Red sails   270
     Wide
     To leeward, swing on the heavy spar.
     The barges wash
     Drifting logs
     Down Greenwich reach
     Past the Isle of Dogs.
          Weialala leia
          Wallala leialala

     Elizabeth and Leicester
     Beating oars   280
     The stern was formed
     A gilded shell
     Red and gold
     The brisk swell

Rippled both shores
Southwest wind
Carried down stream
The peal of bells
White towers

   Weialala leia   290
   Wallala leialala

"Trams and dusty trees.
Highbury bore me. Richmond and Kew
Undid me. By Richmond I raised my knees
Supine on the floor of a narrow canoe."

"My feet are at Moorgate, and my heart
Under my feet. After the event
He wept. He promised 'a new start.'
I made no comment. What should I re-
  sent?"

"On Margate Sands.   300
I can connect
Nothing with nothing.
The broken fingernails of dirty hands.
My people humble people who expect
Nothing."

   la la

To Carthage then I came

Burning burning burning burning
O Lord Thou pluckest me out
O Lord Thou pluckest   310

burning

IV. DEATH BY WATER

PHLEBAS the Phoenician, a fortnight dead,
Forgot the cry of gulls, and the deep sea swell
And the profit and loss.
                            A current under sea
Picked his bones in whispers. As he rose and fell
He passed the stages of his age and youth
Entering the whirlpool.
                            Gentile or Jew   319
O you who turn the wheel and look to windward,
Consider Phlebas, who was once handsome and tall
    as you.

V. WHAT THE THUNDER SAID

AFTER the torchlight red on sweaty faces
After the frosty silence in the gardens
After the agony in stony places
The shouting and the crying
Prison and palace and reverberation
Of thunder of spring over distant mountains
He who was living is now dead
We who were living are now dying
With a little patience   330

Here is no water but only rock
Rock and no water and the sandy road
The road winding above among the mountains
Which are mountains of rock without water
If there were water we should stop and drink
Amongst the rock one cannot stop or think
Sweat is dry and feet are in the sand
If there were only water amongst the rock
Dead mountain mouth of carious teeth that can-
    not spit
Here one can neither stand nor lie nor sit   340
There is not even silence in the mountains
But dry sterile thunder without rain
There is not even solitude in the mountains

But red sullen faces sneer and snarl
From doors of mudcracked houses
                                    If there were water
        And no rock
        If there were rock
        And also water
        And water   350
        A spring
        A pool among the rock
        If there were the sound of water only
        Not the cicada
        And dry grass singing
        But sound of water over a rock
        Where the hermit-thrush sings in the pine trees
        Drip drop drip drop drop drop drop
        But there is no water

Who is the third who walks always beside you?
When I count, there are only you and I together 360
But when I look ahead up the white road
There is always another one walking beside you
Gliding wrapt in a brown mantle, hooded
I do not know whether a man or a woman
—But who is that on the other side of you?

What is that sound high in the air
Murmur of maternal lamentation

Who are those hooded hordes swarming
Over endless plains, stumbling in cracked earth
Ringed by the flat horizon only   370
What is the city over the mountains
Cracks and reforms and bursts in the violet air
Falling towers
Jerusalem Athens Alexandria
Vienna London
Unreal

A woman drew her long black hair out tight
And fiddled whisper music on those strings
And bats with baby faces in the violet light
Whistled, and beat their wings   380
And crawled head downward down a blackened
    wall
And upside down in air were towers
Tolling reminiscent bells, that kept the hours
And voices singing out of empty cisterns and ex-
    hausted wells.

In this decayed hole among the mountains
In the faint moonlight, the grass is singing
Over the tumbled graves, about the chapel
There is the empty chapel, only the wind's home.
It has no windows, and the door swings,

Dry bones can harm no one.   390
Only a cock stood on the rooftree
Co co rico co co rico
In a flash of lightning. Then a damp gust
Bringing rain

Ganga was sunken, and the limp leaves
Waited for rain, while the black clouds
Gathered far distant, over Himavant.
The jungle crouched, humped in silence.
Then spoke the thunder
DA   400
Datta: what have we given?
My friend, blood shaking my heart
The awful daring of a moment's surrender
Which an age of prudence can never retract
By this, and this only, we have existed
Which is not to be found in our obituaries
Or in memories draped by the beneficent spider
Or under seals broken by the lean solicitor
In our empty rooms
DA   410
Dayadhvam: I have heard the key
Turn in the door once and turn once only
We think of the key, each in his prison
Thinking of the key, each confirms a prison

Only at nightfall, aethereal rumours
Revive for a moment a broken Coriolanus
DA
Damyata: The boat responded
Gaily, to the hand expert with sail and oar
The sea was calm, your heart would have re-
 sponded   420
Gaily, when invited, beating obedient
To controlling hands

          I sat upon the shore
Fishing, with the arid plain behind me
Shall I at least set my lands in order?
London Bridge is falling down falling down falling
 down
Poi s'ascose nel foco che gli affina
Quando fiam uti chelidon—O swallow swallow
Le Prince d'Aquitaine à la tour abolie
These fragments I have shored against my ruins 430
Why then Ile fit you. Hieronymo's mad againe.
Datta. Dayadhvam. Damyata.
  Shantih shantih shantih

NOTES ON "THE WASTE LAND"

Not only the title, but the plan and a good deal of the incidental symbolism of the poem were suggested by Miss Jessie L. Weston's book on the Grail legend: *From Ritual to Romance* (Cambridge). Indeed, so deeply am I indebted, Miss Weston's book will elucidate the difficulties of the poem much better than my notes can do; and I recommend it (apart from the great interest of the book itself) to any who think such elucidation of the poem worth the trouble. To another work of anthropology I am indebted in general, one which has influenced our generation profoundly; I mean *The Golden Bough;* I have used especially the two volumes *Adonis, Attis, Osiris.* Anyone who is acquainted with these works will immediately recognise in the poem certain references to vegetation ceremonies.

I. THE BURIAL OF THE DEAD

Line 20. Cf. Ezekiel II, i.

23. Cf. Ecclesiastes XII, v.

31. V. Tristan und Isolde, I, verses 5–8.

42. Id. III, verse 24.

46. I am not familiar with the exact constitution of the Tarot pack of cards, from which I have obviously departed to suit my own convenience. The Hanged Man, a member of the traditional pack, fits my purpose in two ways: because he is associated

in my mind with the Hanged God of Frazer, and because I associate him with the hooded figure in the passage of the disciples to Emmaus in Part V. The Phoenician Sailor and the Merchant appear later; also the "crowds of people," and Death by Water is executed in Part IV. The Man with Three Staves (an authentic member of the Tarot pack) I associate, quite arbitrarily, with the Fisher King himself.

60. Cf. Baudelaire:
"Fourmillante cité, cité pleine de rêves,
"Où le spectre en plein jour raccroche le passant."

63. Cf. Inferno III, 55–57:
        "si lunga tratta
di gente, ch'io non avrei mai creduto
    che morte tanta n'avesse disfatta."

64. Cf. Inferno IV, 25–27:
"Quivi, secondo che per ascoltare,
"non avea pianto, ma' che di sospiri,
"che l'aura eterna facevan tremare."

68. A phenomenon which I have often noticed.

74. Cf. the Dirge in Webster's *White Devil*.

76. V. Baudelaire, Preface to *Fleurs du Mal*.

II. A GAME OF CHESS

77. Cf. *Antony and Cleopatra*, II, ii, l. 190.

92. Laquearia. V. *Aeneid*, I, 726:
    dependent lychni laquearibus aureis incensi,
et noctem flammis funalia vincunt.

98. Sylvan scene. V. Milton, *Paradise Lost*, IV, 140.

99. V. Ovid, *Metamorphoses*, VI, Philomela.

100. Cf. Part III, l. 204.

115. Cf. Part III, l. 195.

118. Cf. Webster: "Is the wind in that door still?"

126. Cf. Part I, l. 37, 48.

138. Cf. the game of chess in Middleton's *Women beware Women*.

III. THE FIRE SERMON

176. V. Spenser, *Prothalamion*.

192. Cf. *The Tempest*, I, ii.

196. Cf. Marvell, *To His Coy Mistress*.

197. Cf. Day, *Parliament of Bees:*
"When of the sudden, listening, you shall hear,
"A noise of horns and hunting, which shall bring
"Actaeon to Diana in the spring,
"Where all shall see her naked skin . . ."

199. I do not know the origin of the ballad from which these lines are taken: it was reported to me from Sydney, Australia.

202. V. Verlaine, *Parsifal*.

210. The currants were quoted at a price "carriage and insurance free to London"; and the Bill of Lading etc. were to be handed to the buyer upon payment of the sight draft.

218. Tiresias, although a mere spectator and not indeed a "character," is yet the most important personage in the poem, uniting all the rest. Just as the one-eyed merchant, seller of currants, melts into the Phoenician Sailor, and the latter is not wholly distinct from Ferdinand Prince of Naples, so all the women are one woman, and the two sexes meet in Tiresias. What Tiresias *sees*, in fact, is the substance of the poem. The whole passage from Ovid is of great anthropological interest:

'. . . Cum Iunone iocos et maior vestra profecto est
Quam, quae contingit maribus,' dixisse, 'voluptas.'
Illa negat; placuit quae sit sententia docti
Quaerere Tiresiae: venus huic erat utraque nota.
Nam duo magnorum viridi coeuntia silva
Corpora serpentum baculi violaverat ictu
Deque viro factus, mirabile, femina septem
Egerat autumnos; octavo rursus eosdem
Vidit et 'est vestrae si tanta potentia plagae,'
Dixit 'ut auctoris sortem in contraria mutet,
Nunc quoque vos feriam!' percussis anguibus isdem
Forma prior rediit genetivaque venit imago.
Arbiter hic igitur sumptus de lite iocosa
Dicta Iovis firmat; gravius Saturnia iusto
Nec pro materia fertur doluisse suique
Iudicis aeterna damnavit lumina nocte,
At pater omnipotens (neque enim licet inrita cuiquam
Facta dei fecisse deo) pro lumine adempto
Scire futura dedit poenamque levavit honore.

221. This may not appear as exact as Sappho's lines, but I had in mind the "longshore" or "dory" fisherman, who returns at nightfall.

253. V. Goldsmith, the song in *The Vicar of Wakefield*.

257. V. *The Tempest*, as above.

264. The interior of St. Magnus Martyr is to my mind one of the finest among Wren's interiors. See *The Proposed Demolition of Nineteen City Churches:* (P. S. King & Son, Ltd.).

266. The Song of the (three) Thames-daughters begins here. From line 292 to 306 inclusive they speak in turn. V. *Götterdämmerung*, III, i: the Rhine-daughters.

279. V. Froude, *Elizabeth*, Vol. I, ch. iv, letter of De Quadra to Philip of Spain:
"In the afternoon we were in a barge, watching the games on the river. (The queen) was alone with Lord Robert and myself on the poop, when they began to talk nonsense, and went so far that Lord Robert at last said, as I was on the spot there was no reason why they should not be married if the queen pleased."

293. Cf. *Purgatorio*, V, 133:
"Ricorditi di me, che son la Pia;
"Siena mi fe', disfecemi Maremma."

307. V. St. Augustine's *Confessions*: "to Carthage then I came, where a cauldron of unholy loves sang all about mine ears."

308. The complete text of the Buddha's Fire Sermon (which corresponds in importance to the Sermon on the Mount) from which these words are taken, will be found translated in the late Henry Clarke Warren's *Buddhism in Translation* (Harvard Oriental Series). Mr. Warren was one of the great pioneers of Buddhist studies in the Occident.

IV. DEATH BY WATER

312. From St. Augustine's *Confessions* again. The collocation of these two representatives of eastern and western asceticism, as the culmination of this part of the poem, is not an accident.

V. WHAT THE THUNDER SAID

In the first part of Part V three themes are employed: the journey to Emmaus, the approach to the Chapel Perilous (see Miss Weston's book) and the present decay of eastern Europe.

357. This is *Turdus aonalaschkae pallasii*, the hermit-thrush which I have heard in Quebec County. Chapman says (*Handbook of Birds of Eastern North America*) "it is most at home in secluded woodland and thickety retreats. . . . Its notes are not remarkable for variety or volume, but in purity and sweetness of tone and exquisite modulation they are unequalled." Its "water-dripping song" is justly celebrated.

360. The following lines were stimulated by the account of one of the Antarctic expeditions (I forget which, but I think one of Shackleton's): it was

related that the party of explorers, at the extremity of their strength, had the constant delusion that there was *one more member* than could actually be counted.

366–76. Cf. Hermann Hesse, *Blick ins Chaos:* "Schon ist halb Europa, schon ist zumindest der halbe Osten Europas auf dem Wege zum Chaos, fährt betrunken im heiligem Wahn am Abgrund entlang und singt dazu, singt betrunken und hymnisch wie Dmitri Karamasoff sang. Ueber diese Lieder lacht der Bürger beleidigt, der Heilige und Seher hört sie mit Tränen."

401. "Datta, dayadhvam, damyata" (Give, sympathise, control). The fable of the meaning of the Thunder is found in the *Brihadaranyaka—Upanishad*, 5, 1. A translation is found in Deussen's *Sechzig Upanishads des Veda*, p. 489.

407. Cf. Webster, *The White Devil*, V, vi:

". . . they'll remarry
Ere the worm pierce your winding-sheet, ere the spider
Make a thin curtain for your epitaphs."

411. Cf. *Inferno*, XXXIII, 46:
"ed io sentii chiavar l'uscio di sotto
all'orribile torre."

Also F. H. Bradley, *Appearance and Reality*, p. 346.
"My external sensations are no less private to myself than are my thoughts or my feelings. In either

case my experience falls within my own circle, a circle closed on the outside; and, with all its elements alike, every sphere is opaque to the others which surround it. . . . In brief, regarded as an existence which appears in a soul, the whole world for each is peculiar and private to that soul."

424. V. Weston: *From Ritual to Romance;* chapter on the Fisher King.

427. V. *Purgatorio,* XXVI, 148.

"'Ara vos prec per aquella valor
'que vos guida al som de l'escalina,
'sovegna vos a temps de ma dolor.'
Poi s'ascose nel foco che gli affina."

428. V. *Pervigilium Veneris.* Cf. Philomela in Parts II and III.

429. V. Gerard de Nerval, Sonnet *El Desdichado.*

431. V. Kyd's *Spanish Tragedy.*

433. Shantih. Repeated as here, a formal ending to an Upanishad. "The Peace which passeth understanding" is our equivalent to this word.

THE HOLLOW MEN
1925

Mistah Kurtz—he dead.

THE HOLLOW MEN

A penny for the Old Guy

I

WE are the hollow men
We are the stuffed men
Leaning together
Headpiece filled with straw. Alas!
Our dried voices, when
We whisper together
Are quiet and meaningless
As wind in dry grass
Or rats' feet over broken glass
In our dry cellar

Shape without form, shade without colour,
Paralysed force, gesture without motion;

Those who have crossed
With direct eyes, to death's other Kingdom
Remember us—if at all—not as lost
Violent souls, but only
As the hollow men
The stuffed men.

II

Eyes I dare not meet in dreams
In death's dream kingdom

These do not appear:
There, the eyes are
Sunlight on a broken column
There, is a tree swinging
And voices are
In the wind's singing
More distant and more solemn
Than a fading star.

Let me be no nearer
In death's dream kingdom
Let me also wear
Such deliberate disguises
Rat's skin, crowskin, crossed staves
In a field
Behaving as the wind behaves
No nearer—

Not that final meeting
In the twilight kingdom

III

This is the dead land
This is cactus land
Here the stone images
Are raised, here they receive
The supplication of a dead man's hand
Under the twinkle of a fading star.

Is it like this
In death's other kingdom
Waking alone
At the hour when we are
Trembling with tenderness
Lips that would kiss
Form prayers to broken stone.

IV

The eyes are not here
There are no eyes here
In this valley of dying stars
In this hollow valley
This broken jaw of our lost kingdoms

In this last of meeting places
We grope together
And avoid speech
Gathered on this beach of the tumid river

Sightless, unless
The eyes reappear
As the perpetual star
Multifoliate rose
Of death's twilight kingdom
The hope only
Of empty men.

V

Here we go round the prickly pear
Prickly pear prickly pear
Here we go round the prickly pear
At five o'clock in the morning.

Between the idea
And the reality
Between the motion
And the act
Falls the Shadow
                    For Thine is the Kingdom

Between the conception
And the creation
Between the emotion
And the response
Falls the Shadow

                         Life is very long

Between the desire
And the spasm
Between the potency
And the existence
Between the essence
And the descent
Falls the Shadow
                    For Thine is the Kingdom

For Thine is
Life is
For Thine is the

This is the way the world ends
This is the way the world ends
This is the way the world ends
Not with a bang but a whimper.

ASH-WEDNESDAY
1930

I

Because I do not hope to turn again
Because I do not hope
Because I do not hope to turn
Desiring this man's gift and that man's scope
I no longer strive to strive towards such things
(Why should the agèd eagle stretch its wings?)
Why should I mourn
The vanished power of the usual reign?

Because I do not hope to know again
The infirm glory of the positive hour
Because I do not think
Because I know I shall not know
The one veritable transitory power
Because I cannot drink
There, where trees flower, and springs flow, for
    there is nothing again

Because I know that time is always time
And place is always and only place
And what is actual is actual only for one time
And only for one place
I rejoice that things are as they are and
I renounce the blessèd face
And renounce the voice

Because I cannot hope to turn again
Consequently I rejoice, having to construct some-
    thing
Upon which to rejoice

And pray to God to have mercy upon us
And I pray that I may forget
These matters that with myself I too much discuss
Too much explain
Because I do not hope to turn again
Let these words answer
For what is done, not to be done again
May the judgement not be too heavy upon us

Because these wings are no longer wings to fly
But merely vans to beat the air
The air which is now thoroughly small and dry
Smaller and dryer than the will
Teach us to care and not to care
Teach us to sit still.

Pray for us sinners now and at the hour of our death
Pray for us now and at the hour of our death.

II

LADY, three white leopards sat under a juniper-tree
In the cool of the day, having fed to satiety
On my legs my heart my liver and that which
    had been contained
In the hollow round of my skull. And God said
Shall these bones live? shall these
Bones live? And that which had been contained
In the bones (which were already dry) said chirping:
Because of the goodness of this Lady
And because of her loveliness, and because
She honours the Virgin in meditation,
We shine with brightness. And I who am here
    dissembled
Proffer my deeds to oblivion, and my love
To the posterity of the desert and the fruit of the
    gourd.
It is this which recovers
My guts the strings of my eyes and the indigestible
    portions
Which the leopards reject. The Lady is withdrawn
In a white gown, to contemplation, in a white gown.
Let the whiteness of bones atone to forgetfulness.
There is no life in them. As I am forgotten
And would be forgotten, so I would forget
Thus devoted, concentrated in purpose. And God
    said

Prophesy to the wind, to the wind only for only
The wind will listen. And the bones sang chirping
With the burden of the grasshopper, saying

Lady of silences
Calm and distressed
Torn and most whole
Rose of memory
Rose of forgetfulness
Exhausted and life-giving
Worried reposeful
The single Rose
Is now the Garden
Where all loves end
Terminate torment
Of love unsatisfied
The greater torment
Of love satisfied
End of the endless
Journey to no end
Conclusion of all that
Is inconclusible
Speech without word and
Word of no speech
Grace to the Mother
For the Garden
Where all love ends.

Under a juniper-tree the bones sang, scattered and
    shining
We are glad to be scattered, we did little good to
    each other,
Under a tree in the cool of the day, with the blessing
    of sand,
Forgetting themselves and each other, united
In the quiet of the desert. This is the land which ye
Shall divide by lot. And neither division nor unity
Matters. This is the land. We have our inheritance.

III

At the first turning of the second stair
I turned and saw below
The same shape twisted on the banister
Under the vapour in the fetid air
Struggling with the devil of the stairs who wears
The deceitful face of hope and of despair.

At the second turning of the second stair
I left them twisting, turning below;
There were no more faces and the stair was dark,
Damp, jaggèd, like an old man's mouth drivelling,
    beyond repair,
Or the toothed gullet of an agèd shark.

At the first turning of the third stair
Was a slotted window bellied like the fig's fruit
And beyond the hawthorn blossom and a pasture
    scene
The broadbacked figure drest in blue and green
Enchanted the maytime with an antique flute.
Blown hair is sweet, brown hair over the mouth
    blown,
Lilac and brown hair;
Distraction, music of the flute, stops and steps of
    the mind over the third stair,

Fading, fading; strength beyond hope and despair
Climbing the third stair.

Lord, I am not worthy
Lord, I am not worthy

      but speak the word only.

IV

Who walked between the violet and the violet
Who walked between
The various ranks of varied green
Going in white and blue, in Mary's colour,
Talking of trivial things
In ignorance and in knowledge of eternal dolour
Who moved among the others as they walked,
Who then made strong the fountains and made
    fresh the springs

Made cool the dry rock and made firm the sand
In blue of larkspur, blue of Mary's colour,
Sovegna vos

Here are the years that walk between, bearing
Away the fiddles and the flutes, restoring
One who moves in the time between sleep and wak-
    ing, wearing

White light folded, sheathed about her, folded.
The new years walk, restoring
Through a bright cloud of tears, the years, restoring
With a new verse the ancient rhyme. Redeem
The time. Redeem
The unread vision in the higher dream
While jewelled unicorns draw by the gilded hearse.

The silent sister veiled in white and blue
Between the yews, behind the garden god,
Whose flute is breathless, bent her head and signed
    but spoke no word

But the fountain sprang up and the bird sang down
Redeem the time, redeem the dream
The token of the word unheard, unspoken

Till the wind shake a thousand whispers from the
    yew

And after this our exile

V

If the lost word is lost, if the spent word is spent
If the unheard, unspoken
Word is unspoken, unheard;
Still is the unspoken word, the Word unheard,
The Word without a word, the Word within
The world and for the world;
And the light shone in darkness and
Against the Word the unstilled world still whirled
About the centre of the silent Word.

O my people, what have I done unto thee.

Where shall the word be found, where will the
    word
Resound? Not here, there is not enough silence
Not on the sea or on the islands, not
On the mainland, in the desert or the rain land,
For those who walk in darkness
Both in the day time and in the night time
The right time and the right place are not here
No place of grace for those who avoid the face
No time to rejoice for those who walk among noise
    and deny the voice

Will the veiled sister pray for
Those who walk in darkness, who chose thee and
    oppose thee,

Those who are torn on the horn between season
    and season, time and time, between
Hour and hour, word and word, power and power,
  · those who wait
In darkness? Will the veiled sister pray
For children at the gate
Who will not go away and cannot pray:
Pray for those who chose and oppose

            O my people, what have I done unto thee.

Will the veiled sister between the slender
Yew trees pray for those who offend her
And are terrified and cannot surrender
And affirm before the world and deny between
    the rocks
In the last desert between the last blue rocks
The desert in the garden the garden in the desert
Of drouth, spitting from the mouth the withered
    apple-seed.

            O my people.

VI

Although I do not hope to turn again
Although I do not hope
Although I do not hope to turn

Wavering between the profit and the loss
In this brief transit where the dreams cross
The dreamcrossed twilight between birth and
    dying
(Bless me father) though I do not wish to wish
    these things
From the wide window towards the granite shore
The white sails still fly seaward, seaward flying
Unbroken wings

And the lost heart stiffens and rejoices
In the lost lilac and the lost sea voices
And the weak spirit quickens to rebel
For the bent golden-rod and the lost sea smell
Quickens to recover
The cry of quail and the whirling plover
And the blind eye creates
The empty forms between the ivory gates
And smell renews the salt savour of the sandy earth

This is the time of tension between dying and birth
The place of solitude where three dreams cross

Between blue rocks
But when the voices shaken from the yew-tree drift
    away
Let the other yew be shaken and reply.

Blessèd sister, holy mother, spirit of the fountain,
    spirit of the garden,
Suffer us not to mock ourselves with falsehood
Teach us to care and not to care
Teach us to sit still
Even among these rocks,
Our peace in His will
And even among these rocks
Sister, mother
And spirit of the river, spirit of the sea,
Suffer me not to be separated

And let my cry come unto Thee.

ARIEL POEMS

JOURNEY OF THE MAGI

'A COLD coming we had of it,
Just the worst time of the year
For a journey, and such a long journey:
The ways deep and the weather sharp,
The very dead of winter.'
And the camels galled, sore-footed, refractory,
Lying down in the melting snow.
There were times we regretted
The summer palaces on slopes, the terraces,
And the silken girls bringing sherbet.
Then the camel men cursing and grumbling
And running away, and wanting their liquor and
        women,
And the night-fires going out, and the lack of
        shelters,
And the cities hostile and the towns unfriendly
And the villages dirty and charging high prices:
A hard time we had of it.
At the end we preferred to travel all night,
Sleeping in snatches,
With the voices singing in our ears, saying
That this was all folly.

Then at dawn we came down to a temperate valley,
Wet, below the snow line, smelling of vegetation;

With a running stream and a water-mill beating
    the darkness,
And three trees on the low sky,
And an old white horse galloped away in the
    meadow.
Then we came to a tavern with vine-leaves over
    the lintel,
Six hands at an open door dicing for pieces of silver,
And feet kicking the empty wine-skins.
But there was no information, and so we continued
And arrived at evening, not a moment too soon
Finding the place; it was (you may say) satisfactory.

All this was a long time ago, I remember,
And I would do it again, but set down
This set down
This: were we led all that way for
Birth or Death? There was a Birth, certainly,
We had evidence and no doubt. I had seen birth
    and death,
But had thought they were different; this Birth was
Hard and bitter agony for us, like Death, our death.
We returned to our places, these Kingdoms,
But no longer at ease here, in the old dispensation,
With an alien people clutching their gods.
I should be glad of another death.

A SONG FOR SIMEON

LORD, the Roman hyacinths are blooming in bowls
    and
The winter sun creeps by the snow hills;
The stubborn season has made stand.
My life is light, waiting for the death wind,
Like a feather on the back of my hand.
Dust in sunlight and memory in corners
Wait for the wind that chills towards the dead land.

Grant us thy peace.
I have walked many years in this city,
Kept faith and fast, provided for the poor,
Have given and taken honour and ease.
There went never any rejected from my door.
Who shall remember my house, where shall live
    my children's children
When the time of sorrow is come?
They will take to the goat's path, and the fox's home,
Fleeing from the foreign faces and the foreign
    swords.

Before the time of cords and scourges and lamenta-
    tion
Grant us thy peace.
Before the stations of the mountain of desolation,
Before the certain hour of maternal sorrow,

Now at this birth season of decease,
Let the Infant, the still unspeaking and unspoken
    Word,
Grant Israel's consolation
To one who has eighty years and no to-morrow.

According to thy word.
They shall praise Thee and suffer in every genera-
    tion
With glory and derision,
Light upon light, mounting the saints' stair.
Not for me the martyrdom, the ecstasy of thought
    and prayer,
Not for me the ultimate vision.
Grant me thy peace.
(And a sword shall pierce thy heart,
Thine also.)
I am tired with my own life and the lives of those
    after me,
I am dying in my own death and the deaths of
    those after me.
Let thy servant depart,
Having seen thy salvation.

ANIMULA

'Issues from the hand of God, the simple soul'
To a flat world of changing lights and noise,
To light, dark, dry or damp, chilly or warm;
Moving between the legs of tables and of chairs,
Rising or falling, grasping at kisses and toys,
Advancing boldly, sudden to take alarm,
Retreating to the corner of arm and knee,
Eager to be reassured, taking pleasure
In the fragrant brilliance of the Christmas tree,
Pleasure in the wind, the sunlight and the sea;
Studies the sunlit pattern on the floor
And running stags around a silver tray;
Confounds the actual and the fanciful,
Content with playing-cards and kings and queens,
What the fairies do and what the servants say.
The heavy burden of the growing soul
Perplexes and offends more, day by day;
Week by week, offends and perplexes more
With the imperatives of 'is and seems'
And may and may not, desire and control.
The pain of living and the drug of dreams
Curl up the small soul in the window seat
Behind the *Encyclopædia Britannica*.
Issues from the hand of time the simple soul
Irresolute and selfish, misshapen, lame,
Unable to fare forward or retreat,

Fearing the warm reality, the offered good,
Denying the importunity of the blood,
Shadow of its own shadows, spectre in its own
    gloom,
Leaving disordered papers in a dusty room;
Living first in the silence after the viaticum.

Pray for Guiterriez, avid of speed and power,
For Boudin, blown to pieces,
For this one who made a great fortune,
And that one who went his own way.
Pray for Floret, by the boarhound slain between
    the yew trees,
Pray for us now and at the hour of our birth.

MARINA

Quis hic locus, quae regio, quae mundi plaga?

WHAT seas what shores what grey rocks and what
    islands
What water lapping the bow
And scent of pine and the woodthrush singing
    through the fog
What images return
O my daughter.

Those who sharpen the tooth of the dog, meaning
Death
Those who glitter with the glory of the humming-
    bird, meaning
Death
Those who sit in the stye of contentment, meaning
Death
Those who suffer the ecstasy of the animals, mean-
    ing
Death

Are become unsubstantial, reduced by a wind,
A breath of pine, and the woodsong fog
By this grace dissolved in place

What is this face, less clear and clearer
The pulse in the arm, less strong and stronger—

Given or lent? more distant than stars and nearer
    than the eye

Whispers and small laughter between leaves and
    hurrying feet
Under sleep, where all the waters meet.

Bowsprit cracked with ice and paint cracked with
    heat.
I made this, I have forgotten
And remember.
The rigging weak and the canvas rotten
Between one June and another September.
Made this unknowing, half conscious, unknown,
    my own.
The garboard strake leaks, the seams need caulking.
This form, this face, this life
Living to live in a world of time beyond me; let me
Resign my life for this life, my speech for that un-
    spoken,
The awakened, lips parted, the hope, the new ships.

What seas what shores what granite islands towards
    my timbers
And woodthrush calling through the fog
My daughter.

UNFINISHED POEMS

SWEENEY AGONISTES

FRAGMENTS OF AN
ARISTOPHANIC MELODRAMA

ORESTES: You don't see them, you don't—but *I* see them: they are hunting me down, I must move on.—*Choephoroi.*

Hence the soul cannot be possessed of the divine union, until it has divested itself of the love of created beings.—*St. John of the Cross.*

FRAGMENT OF A PROLOGUE

DUSTY. DORIS.

DUSTY: How about Pereira?

DORIS: What about Pereira?
I don't care.

DUSTY: You don't care!
Who pays the rent?

DORIS: Yes he pays the rent

DUSTY: Well some men don't and some men do
Some men don't and you know who

DORIS: You can have Pereira

DUSTY: What about Pereira?

DORIS: He's no gentleman, Pereira:
You can't trust him!

DUSTY: Well that's true.
He's no gentleman if you can't trust him
And *if* you can't trust him—
Then you never know what he's going to do.

DORIS: No it wouldn't do to be too nice to Pereira.

DUSTY: Now Sam's a gentleman through and
through.

DORIS: I like Sam

DUSTY: *I* like Sam
Yes and Sam's a nice boy too.
He's a funny fellow

DORIS: He *is* a funny fellow
         He's like a fellow once I knew.
         He could make you laugh.
DUSTY: Sam can make you laugh:
         Sam's all right
DORIS: But Pereira won't do.
         We can't have Pereira
DUSTY: Well what you going to do?
TELEPHONE: Ting a ling ling
                    Ting a ling ling
DUSTY: That's Pereira
DORIS: Yes that's Pereira
DUSTY: Well what you going to do?
TELEPHONE: Ting a ling ling
                    Ting a ling ling
DUSTY: That's Pereira
DORIS: Well can't you stop that horrible noise?
         Pick up the receiver
DUSTY: What'll I say!
DORIS: Say what you like: say I'm ill,
         Say I broke my leg on the stairs
         Say we've had a fire
DUSTY: Hello Hello are you there?
         Yes this is Miss Dorrance's *flat*—
         Oh Mr. Pereira is that you? how do you do!
         Oh I'm *so* sorry. I *am* so sorry

138

But Doris came home with a terrible chill
No, just a chill
Oh I *think* it's only a chill
Yes indeed I hope so too—
Well I *hope* we shan't have to call a doctor
Doris just hates having a doctor
She says will you ring up on Monday
She hopes to be all right on Monday
I say do you mind if I ring off now
She's got her feet in mustard and water
I said I'm giving her mustard and water
All right, Monday you'll phone through.
Yes I'll tell her. Good bye. Goooood bye.
I'm sure, that's very kind of *you.*

Ah-h-h

DORIS: Now I'm going to cut the cards for to-night.
      Oh guess what the first is

DUSTY: First is. What is?

DORIS: The King of Clubs

DUSTY: That's Pereira

DORIS: It might be Sweeney

DUSTY: It's Pereira

DORIS: It might *just* as well be Sweeney

DUSTY: Well anyway it's very queer.

DORIS: Here's the four of diamonds, what's that
      mean?

DUSTY [reading]: 'A small sum of money, or a present
Of wearing apparel, or a party.'
That's queer too.

DORIS: Here's the three. What's that mean?

DUSTY: 'News of an absent friend.'—Pereira!

DORIS: The Queen of Hearts!—Mrs. Porter!

DUSTY: Or it might be you

DORIS: Or it might be you
We're all hearts. You can't be sure.
It just depends on what comes next.
You've got to *think* when you read the cards,
It's not a thing that anyone can do.

DUSTY: Yes I know you've a touch with the cards
What comes next?

DORIS: What comes next. It's the six.

DUSTY: 'A quarrel. An estrangement. Separation of friends.'

DORIS: Here's the two of spades.

DUSTY: The *two* of *spades!*
THAT'S THE COFFIN!!

DORIS: THAT'S THE COFFIN?
Oh good heavens what'll I do?
Just before a party too!

DUSTY: Well it needn't be yours, it may mean a friend.

DORIS: No it's mine. I'm sure it's mine.

I dreamt of weddings all last night.

Yes it's mine. I know it's mine.

Oh good heavens what'll I do.

Well I'm not going to draw any more,

You cut for luck. You cut for luck.

It might break the spell. You cut for luck.

DUSTY: The Knave of Spades.

DORIS: That'll be Snow

DUSTY: Or it might be Swarts

DORIS: Or it might be Snow

DUSTY: It's a funny thing how I draw court cards —

DORIS: There's a lot in the way you pick them up

DUSTY: There's an awful lot in the way you feel

DORIS: Sometimes they'll tell you nothing at all

DUSTY: You've got to know what you want to ask
            them

DORIS: You've got to know what you want to know

DUSTY: It's no use asking them too much

DORIS: It's no use asking more than once

DUSTY: Sometimes they're no use at all.

DORIS: I'd like to know about that coffin.

DUSTY: Well I never! What did I tell you?

Wasn't I saying I always draw court cards?

The Knave of Hearts!

[Whistle outside of the window.]

·141·

Well I *never*

What a co*in*cidence! Cards are queer!

[Whistle again.]

DORIS: Is that Sam?

DUSTY: Of course it's Sam!

DORIS: Of course, the Knave of Hearts *is* Sam!

DUSTY *[leaning out of the window]*: Hello Sam!

WAUCHOPE: Hello dear
How many's up there?

DUSTY: Nobody's up here
How many's down there?

WAUCHOPE: Four of us here.
Wait till I put the car round the corner
We'll be right up

DUSTY: All right, come up.

DUSTY *[to* DORIS]: Cards are queer.

DORIS: I'd like to know about that coffin.

KNOCK KNOCK KNOCK

KNOCK KNOCK KNOCK

KNOCK

KNOCK

KNOCK

DORIS. DUSTY. WAUCHOPE. HORSFALL. KLIPSTEIN.

KRUMPACKER.

WAUCHOPE: Hello Doris! Hello Dusty! How do
you do!

142

How come? how come? will you permit
　　me—
I think you girls both know Captain Hors-
　　fall—
We want you to meet two friends of ours,
American gentlemen here on business.
Meet Mr. Klipstein. Meet Mr. Krumpacker.

KLIPSTEIN: How do you do

KRUMPACKER:　　　　How do you do

KLIPSTEIN: I'm very pleased to make your ac-
　　quaintance

KRUMPACKER: Extremely pleased to become ac-
　　quainted

KLIPSTEIN: Sam—I should say Loot Sam Wau-
　　chope

KRUMPACKER: Of the Canadian Expeditionary
　　Force—

KLIPSTEIN: The Loot has told us a lot about you.

KRUMPACKER: We were all in the war together
　　Klip and me and the Cap and Sam.

KLIPSTEIN: Yes we did our bit, as you folks
　　say,
　　I'll tell the world we got the Hun on the
　　run

KRUMPACKER: What about that poker game? eh
what Sam?

What about that poker game in Bor-
deaux?

Yes Miss Dorrance you get Sam

To tell about that poker game in Bor-
deaux.

DUSTY: Do you know London well, Mr. Krumpacker?

KLIPSTEIN: No we never been here before

KRUMPACKER: We hit this town last night for the
first time

KLIPSTEIN: And I certainly hope it won't be the
last time.

DORIS: You like London, Mr. Klipstein?

KRUMPACKER: Do we like London? do we like London!

Do we like London!! Eh what Klip?

KLIPSTEIN: Say, Miss—er—uh—London's swell.
We like London fine.

KRUMPACKER: Perfectly slick.

DUSTY: Why don't you come and live here then?

KLIPSTEIN: Well, no, Miss—er—you haven't
quite got it

(I'm afraid I didn't quite catch your name—

144

But I'm very pleased to meet you all the
     same)—
London's a little too gay for us
Yes I'll say a little too gay.
KRUMPACKER: Yes London's a little too gay for us
    Don't think I mean anything *coarse*—
    But I'm afraid we couldn't stand the pace.
    What about it Klip?
KLIPSTEIN: You said it, Krum.
    London's a slick place, London's a swell
     place,
    London's a fine place to come on a visit—
KRUMPACKER: Specially when you got a real live
     Britisher
    A guy like Sam to show you around.
    Sam of course is at *home* in London,
    And he's promised to show us around.

FRAGMENT OF AN AGON

SWEENEY. WAUCHOPE. HORSFALL. KLIPSTEIN.
KRUMPACKER. SWARTS. SNOW. DORIS. DUSTY.

SWEENEY: I'll carry you off
            To a cannibal isle.

DORIS: You'll be the cannibal!

SWEENEY: You'll be the missionary!
            You'll be my little seven stone mission-
               ary!
            I'll gobble you up. I'll be the cannibal.

DORIS: You'll carry me off? To a cannibal isle?

SWEENEY: I'll be the cannibal.

DORIS: I'll be the missionary.
            I'll convert you!

SWEENEY: I'll convert *you!*
            Into a stew.
            A nice little, white little, missionary stew.

DORIS: You wouldn't eat me!

SWEENEY: Yes I'd eat you!
            In a nice little, white little, soft little, ten-
               der little,
            Juicy little, right little, missionary stew.
            You see this egg
            You see this egg
            Well that's life on a crocodile isle.

There's no telephones
There's no gramophones
There's no motor cars
No two-seaters, no six-seaters,
No Citroën, no Rolls-Royce.
Nothing to eat but the fruit as it grows.
Nothing to see but the palmtrees one way
And the sea the other way,
Nothing to hear but the sound of the surf.
Nothing at all but three things

DORIS: What things?

SWEENEY: Birth, and copulation, and death.
That's all, that's all, that's all, that's all,
Birth, and copulation, and death.

DORIS: I'd be bored.

SWEENEY: You'd be bored.
Birth, and copulation, and death.

DORIS: I'd be bored.

SWEENEY: You'd be bored.
Birth, and copulation, and death.
That's all the facts when you come to
          brass tacks:
Birth, and copulation, and death.
I've been born, and once is enough.
You dont remember, but I remember,
Once is enough.

SONG BY WAUCHOPE AND HORSFALL
SWARTS AS TAMBO. SNOW AS BONES

Under the bamboo
Bamboo bamboo
Under the bamboo tree
Two live as one
One live as two
Two live as three
Under the bam
Under the boo
Under the bamboo tree.

Where the breadfruit fall
And the penguin call
And the sound is the sound of the sea
Under the bam
Under the boo
Under the bamboo tree.

Where the Gauguin maids
In the banyan shades
Wear palmleaf drapery
Under the bam
Under the boo
Under the bamboo tree.

Tell me in what part of the wood
Do you want to flirt with me?
Under the breadfruit, banyan, palmleaf
Or under the bamboo tree?
Any old tree will do for me
Any old wood is just as good
Any old isle is just my style
Any fresh egg
Any fresh egg
And the sound of the coral sea.

DORIS: I dont like eggs; I never liked eggs;
And I dont like life on your crocodile isle.

SONG BY KLIPSTEIN AND KRUMPACKER
SNOW AND SWARTS AS BEFORE

My little island girl
My little island girl
I'm going to stay with you
And we wont worry what to do
We wont have to catch any trains
And we wont go home when it rains
We'll gather hibiscus flowers
For it wont be minutes but hours
For it wont be hours but years

	And the morning
	And the evening
	And noontime
diminuendo	*And night*
	Morning
	Evening
	Noontime
	Night

DORIS: That's not life, that's no life
Why I'd just as soon be dead.

SWEENEY: That's what life is. Just is

DORIS: What is?
What's that life is?

SWEENEY: Life is death.
I knew a man once did a girl in—

DORIS: Oh Mr. Sweeney, please dont talk,
I cut the cards before you came
And I drew the coffin

SWARTS: *You* drew the coffin?

DORIS: I drew the COFFIN very last card.
I dont care for such conversation
A woman runs a terrible risk.

SNOW: Let Mr. Sweeney continue his story.
I assure you, Sir, we are very interested.

SWEENEY: I knew a man once did a girl in
Any man might do a girl in

Any man has to, needs to, wants to
Once in a lifetime, do a girl in.
Well he kept her there in a bath
With a gallon of lysol in a bath

SWARTS: These fellows always get pinched in the
end.

SNOW: Excuse me, they dont all get pinched in
the end.

What about them bones on Epsom
Heath?
I seen that in the papers
You seen it in the papers
They *dont* all get pinched in the end.

DORIS: A woman runs a terrible risk.

SNOW: Let Mr. Sweeney continue his story.

SWEENEY: This one didn't get pinched in the end
But that's another story too.
This went on for a couple of months
Nobody came
And nobody went
But he took in the milk and he paid the
rent.

SWARTS: What did he do?
All that time, what did he do?

SWEENEY: What did he do! what did he do?
That dont apply.

151

Talk to live men about what they do.
He used to come and see me sometimes
I'd give him a drink and cheer him up.
DORIS: Cheer him up?
DUSTY: Cheer him up?
SWEENEY: Well here again that dont apply
But I've gotta use words when I talk to
    you.
But here's what I was going to say.
He didn't know if he was alive
          and the girl was dead
He didn't know if the girl was alive
          and he was dead
He didn't know if they both were alive
          or both were dead
If he was alive then the milkman wasn't
          and the rent-collector wasn't
And if they were alive then he was dead.
There wasn't any joint
There wasn't any joint
For when you're alone
When you're alone like he was alone
You're either or neither
I tell you again it dont apply
Death or life or life or death
Death is life and life is death

I gotta use words when I talk to you
But if you understand or if you dont
That's nothing to me and nothing to you
We all gotta do what we gotta do
We're gona sit here and drink this booze
We're gona sit here and have a tune
We're gona stay and we're gona go
And somebody's gotta pay the rent
DORIS: I know who
SWEENEY: But that's nothing to me and nothing to
      you.

FULL CHORUS: WAUCHOPE, HORSFALL, KLIPSTEIN,
            KRUMPACKER

When you're alone in the middle of the night
      and you wake in a sweat and a hell of a fright
When you're alone in the middle of the bed and
      you wake like someone hit you on the head
You've had a cream of a nightmare dream and
      you've got the hoo-ha's coming to you.
Hoo hoo hoo
You dreamt you waked up at seven o'clock and
      it's foggy and it's damp and it's dawn and
      it's dark
And you wait for a knock and the turning of a
      lock for you know the hangman's waiting for
      you.

And perhaps you're alive
And perhaps you're dead
Hoo ha ha
Hoo ha ha
Hoo
Hoo
Hoo
Knock Knock Knock
Knock Knock Knock
Knock
Knock
Knock

CORIOLAN

I. TRIUMPHAL MARCH

Stone, bronze, stone, steel, stone, oakleaves horses'
    heels
Over the paving.
And the flags. And the trumpets. And so many
    eagles.
How many? Count them. And such a press of
    people.
We hardly knew ourselves that day, or knew the
    City.
This is the way to the temple, and we so many
    crowding the way.
So many waiting, how many waiting? what did it
    matter, on such a day?
Are they coming? No, not yet. You can see some
    eagles. And hear the trumpets.
Here they come. Is he coming?
The natural wakeful life of our Ego is a perceiving.
We can wait with our stools and our sausages.
What comes first? Can you see? Tell us. It is

    5,800,000 rifles and carbines,
      102,000 machine guns,
       28,000 trench mortars,
       53,000 field and heavy guns,
I cannot tell how many projectiles, mines and fuses,

157

                    13,000 aeroplanes,
                    24,000 aeroplane engines,
                    50,000 ammunition waggons,
            now 55,000 army waggons,
                    11,000 field kitchens,
                    1,150 field bakeries.

What a time that took. Will it be he now? No,
Those are the golf club Captains, these the Scouts,
And now the *société gymnastique de Poissy*
And now come the Mayor and the Liverymen.
    Look
There he is now, look:
There is no interrogation in his eyes
Or in the hands, quiet over the horse's neck,
And the eyes watchful, waiting, perceiving, in-
    different.
O hidden under the dove's wing, hidden in the
    turtle's breast,
Under the palmtree at noon, under the running
    water
At the still point of the turning world. O hidden.

Now they go up to the temple. Then the sacrifice.
Now come the virgins bearing urns, urns contain-
    ing

Dust
Dust
Dust of dust, and now
Stone, bronze, stone, steel, stone, oakleaves, horses'
    heels
Over the paving.

That is all we could see. But how many eagles! and
    how many trumpets!
(And Easter Day, we didn't get to the country,
So we took young Cyril to church. And they
    rang a bell
And he said right out loud, *crumpets*.)
                    Don't throw away that sausage,
It'll come in handy. He's artful. Please, will you
Give us a light?
Light
Light
*Et les soldats faisaient la haie? ILS LA FAI–
    SAIENT.*

II. DIFFICULTIES
OF A STATESMAN

CRY what shall I cry?
All flesh is grass: comprehending
The Companions of the Bath, the Knights of the
    British Empire, the Cavaliers,
O Cavaliers! of the Legion of Honour,
The Order of the Black Eagle (1st and 2nd class),
And the Order of the Rising Sun.
Cry cry what shall I cry?
The first thing to do is to form the committees:
The consultative councils, the standing committees,
    select committees and sub-committees.
One secretary will do for several committees.
What shall I cry?
Arthur Edward Cyril Parker is appointed telephone
    operator
At a salary of one pound ten a week rising by an-
    nual increments of five shillings
To two pounds ten a week; with a bonus of thirty
    shillings at Christmas
And one week's leave a year.
A committee has been appointed to nominate a com-
    mission of engineers
To consider the Water Supply.

A commission is appointed
For Public Works, chiefly the question of rebuild-
ing the fortifications.
A commission is appointed
To confer with a Volscian commission
About perpetual peace: the fletchers and javelin-
makers and smiths
Have appointed a joint committee to protest against
the reduction of orders.
Meanwhile the guards shake dice on the marshes
And the frogs (O Mantuan) croak in the marshes.
Fireflies flare against the faint sheet lightning
What shall I cry?
Mother mother
Here is the row of family portraits, dingy busts, all
looking remarkably Roman,
Remarkably like each other, lit up successively by
the flare
Of a sweaty torchbearer, yawning.
O hidden under the ... Hidden under the ...
Where the dove's foot rested and locked for a
moment,
A still moment, repose of noon, set under the upper
branches of noon's widest tree
Under the breast feather stirred by the small wind
after noon

There the cyclamen spreads its wings, there the
    clematis droops over the lintel
O mother (not among these busts, all correctly
    inscribed)
I a tired head among these heads
Necks strong to bear them
Noses strong to break the wind
Mother
May we not be some time, almost now, together,
If the mactations, immolations, oblations, impetra-
    tions,
Are now observed
May we not be
O hidden
Hidden in the stillness of noon, in the silent croak-
    ing night.
Come with the sweep of the little bat's wing, with
    the small flare of the firefly or lightning bug,
"Rising and falling, crowned with dust," the small
    creatures,
The small creatures chirp thinly through the dust,
    through the night.
O mother
What shall I cry?
We demand a committee, a representative com-
    mittee, a committee of investigation

      RESIGN   RESIGN   RESIGN

MINOR POEMS

EYES THAT LAST I SAW
IN TEARS

Eyes that last I saw in tears
Through division
Here in death's dream kingdom
The golden vision reappears
I see the eyes but not the tears
This is my affliction

This is my affliction
Eyes I shall not see again
Eyes of decision
Eyes I shall not see unless
At the door of death's other kingdom
Where, as in this,
The eyes outlast a little while
A little while outlast the tears
And hold us in derision.

THE WIND SPRANG UP
AT FOUR O'CLOCK

THE wind sprang up at four o'clock
The wind sprang up and broke the bells
Swinging between life and death
Here, in death's dream kingdom
The waking echo of confusing strife
Is it a dream or something else
When the surface of the blackened river
Is a face that sweats with tears?
I saw across the blackened river
The camp fire shake with alien spears.
Here, across death's other river
The Tartar horsemen shake their spears.

FIVE-FINGER EXERCISES

I. *Lines to a Persian Cat*

THE songsters of the air repair
To the green fields of Russell Square.
Beneath the trees there is no ease
For the dull brain, the sharp desires
And the quick eyes of Woolly Bear.
There is no relief but in grief.
O when will the creaking heart cease?
When will the broken chair give ease?
Why will the summer day delay?
When will Time flow away?

II. *Lines to a Yorkshire Terrier*

In a brown field stood a tree
And the tree was crookt and dry.
In a black sky, from a green cloud
Natural forces shriek'd aloud,
Screamed, rattled, muttered endlessly.
Little dog was safe and warm
Under a cretonne eiderdown,
Yet the field was cracked and brown
And the tree was cramped and dry.
Pollicle dogs and cats all must
Jellicle cats and dogs all must
Like undertakers, come to dust.

Here a little dog I pause
Heaving up my prior paws,
Pause, and sleep endlessly.

III. *Lines to a Duck in the Park*

The long light shakes across the lake,
The forces of the morning quake,
The dawn is slant across the lawn,
Here is no eft or mortal snake
But only sluggish duck and drake.
I have seen the morning shine,
I have had the Bread and Wine,
Let the feathered mortals take
That which is their mortal due,
Pinching bread and finger too,
Easier had than squirming worm;
For I know, and so should you
That soon the enquiring worm shall try
Our well-preserved complacency.

IV. *Lines to Ralph Hodgson Esqre.*

How delightful to meet Mr. Hodgson!
              (Everyone wants to know *him*)—
With his musical sound
And his Baskerville Hound
Which, just at a word from his master

Will follow you faster and faster
And tear you limb from limb.
How delightful to meet Mr. Hodgson!
Who is worshipped by all waitresses
(They regard him as something apart)
While on his palate fine he presses
The juice of the gooseberry tart.
How delightful to meet Mr. Hodgson!
              (Everyone wants to know *him*).
He has 999 canaries
And round his head finches and fairies
In jubilant rapture skim.
How delightful to meet Mr. Hodgson!
              (Everyone wants to meet *him*).

V. *Lines for Cuscuscaraway and Mirza*
        Murad Ali Beg

How unpleasant to meet Mr. Eliot!
With his features of clerical cut,
And his brow so grim
And his mouth so prim
And his conversation, so nicely
Restricted to What Precisely
And If and Perhaps and But.
How unpleasant to meet Mr. Eliot!
With a bobtail cur

In a coat of fur
And a porpentine cat
And a wopsical hat:
How unpleasant to meet Mr. Eliot!
       (Whether his mouth be open or shut).

LANDSCAPES

I. *New Hampshire*

CHILDREN's voices in the orchard
Between the blossom- and the fruit-time:
Golden head, crimson head,
Between the green tip and the root.
Black wing, brown wing, hover over;
Twenty years and the spring is over;
To-day grieves, to-morrow grieves,
Cover me over, light-in-leaves;
Golden head, black wing,
Cling, swing,
Spring, sing,
Swing up into the apple-tree.

II. *Virginia*

Red river, red river,
Slow flow heat is silence
No will is still as a river
Still. Will heat move
Only through the mocking-bird
Heard once? Still hills
Wait. Gates wait. Purple trees,
White trees, wait, wait,
Delay, decay. Living, living,
Never moving. Ever moving
Iron thoughts came with me
And go with me:
Red river, river, river.

III. *Usk*

Do not suddenly break the branch, or
Hope to find
The white hart behind the white well.
Glance aside, not for lance, do not spell
Old enchantments. Let them sleep.
"Gently dip, but not too deep,"
Lift your eyes
Where the roads dip and where the roads rise
Seek only there
Where the grey light meets the green air
The hermit's chapel, the pilgrim's prayer.

IV. *Rannoch, by Glencoe*

Here the crow starves, here the patient stag
Breeds for the rifle. Between the soft moor
And the soft sky, scarcely room
To leap or soar. Substance crumbles, in the thin air
Moon cold or moon hot. The road winds in
Listlessness of ancient war
Languor of broken steel,
Clamour of confused wrong, apt
In silence. Memory is strong
Beyond the bone. Pride snapped,
Shadow of pride is long, in the long pass
No concurrence of bone.

V. *Cape Ann*

O quick quick quick, quick hear the song-sparrow,
Swamp-sparrow, fox-sparrow, vesper-sparrow
At dawn and dusk. Follow the dance
Of the goldfinch at noon. Leave to chance
The Blackburnian warbler, the shy one. Hail
With shrill whistle the note of the quail, the bob-
    white
Dodging by bay-bush. Follow the feet
Of the walker, the water-thrush. Follow the flight
Of the dancing arrow, the purple martin. Greet
In silence the bullbat. All are delectable. Sweet
    sweet sweet
But resign this land at the end, resign it
To its true owner, the tough one, the sea-gull.
The palaver is finished.

LINES FOR AN OLD MAN

THE tiger in the tiger-pit
Is not more irritable than I.
The whipping tail is not more still
Than when I smell the enemy
Writhing in the essential blood
Or dangling from the friendly tree.
When I lay bare the tooth of wit
The hissing over the archèd tongue
Is more affectionate than hate,
More bitter than the love of youth,
And inaccessible by the young.
Reflected from my golden eye
The dullard knows that he is mad.
Tell me if I am not glad!

CHORUSES FROM ''THE ROCK''

I

The Eagle soars in the summit of Heaven,
The Hunter with his dogs pursues his circuit.
O perpetual revolution of configured stars,
O perpetual recurrence of determined seasons,
O world of spring and autumn, birth and dying!
The endless cycle of idea and action,
Endless invention, endless experiment,
Brings knowledge of motion, but not of stillness;
Knowledge of speech, but not of silence;
Knowledge of words, and ignorance of the
    Word.
All our knowledge brings us nearer to our igno-
    rance,
All our ignorance brings us nearer to death,
But nearness to death no nearer to GOD.
Where is the Life we have lost in living?
Where is the wisdom we have lost in knowl-
    edge?
Where is the knowledge we have lost in infor-
    mation?
The cycles of Heaven in twenty centuries
Bring us farther from GOD and nearer to the
    Dust.

I journeyed to London, to the timekept City,
Where the River flows, with foreign flotations.

There I was told: we have too many churches,
And too few chop-houses. There I was told:
Let the vicars retire. Men do not need the Church
In the place where they work, but where they
    spend their Sundays.
In the City, we need no bells:
Let them waken the suburbs.
I journeyed to the suburbs, and there I was told:
We toil for six days, on the seventh we must
    motor
To Hindhead, or Maidenhead.
If the weather is foul we stay at home and read
    the papers.
In industrial districts, there I was told
Of economic laws.
In the pleasant countryside, there it seemed
That the country now is only fit for picnics.
And the Church does not seem to be wanted
In country or in suburb; and in the town
Only for important weddings.

CHORUS LEADER:
    Silence! and preserve respectful distance.
    For I perceive approaching
    The Rock. Who will perhaps answer our doubt-
        ings.

The Rock. The Watcher. The Stranger.
He who has seen what has happened.
And who sees what is to happen.
The Witness. The Critic. The Stranger.
The God-shaken, in whom is the truth inborn.

Enter the ROCK, *led by a* BOY:

THE ROCK:

The lot of man is ceaseless labour,
Or ceaseless idleness, which is still harder,
Or irregular labour, which is not pleasant.
I have trodden the winepress alone, and I know
That it is hard to be really useful, resigning
The things that men count for happiness, seeking
The good deeds that lead to obscurity, accepting
With equal face those that bring ignominy,
The applause of all or the love of none.
All men are ready to invest their money
But most expect dividends.
I say to you: *Make perfect your will.*
I say: take no thought of the harvest,
But only of proper sowing.

The world turns and the world changes,
But one thing does not change.
In all of my years, one thing does not change.

However you disguise it, this thing does not
    change:
The perpetual struggle of Good and Evil.
Forgetful, you neglect your shrines and churches;
The men you are in these times deride
What has been done of good, you find expla-
    nations
To satisfy the rational and enlightened mind.
Second, you neglect and belittle the desert.
The desert is not remote in southern tropics,
The desert is not only around the corner,
The desert is squeezed in the tube-train next to
    you,
The desert is in the heart of your brother.
The good man is the builder, if he build what
    is good.
I will show you the things that are now being
    done,
And some of the things that were long ago done,
That you may take heart. Make perfect your
    will.
Let me show you the work of the humble.
    Listen.

The lights fade; in the semi-darkness the voices of
WORKMEN *are heard chanting.*
  In the vacant places
  We will build with new bricks

There are hands and machines
And clay for new brick
And lime for new mortar
Where the bricks are fallen
We will build with new stone
Where the beams are rotten
We will build with new timbers
Where the word is unspoken
We will build with new speech
There is work together
A Church for all
And a job for each
Every man to his work.

Now a group of WORKMEN is silhouetted against
the dim sky. From farther away, they are answered
by voices of the UNEMPLOYED.
No man has hired us
With pocketed hands
And lowered faces
We stand about in open places
And shiver in unlit rooms.
Only the wind moves
Over empty fields, untilled
Where the plough rests, at an angle
To the furrow. In this land

There shall be one cigarette to two men,
To two women one half pint of bitter
Ale. In this land
No man has hired us.
Our life is unwelcome, our death
Unmentioned in "The Times."

Chant of WORKMEN again.
The river flows, the seasons turn,
The sparrow and starling have no time to waste.
If men do not build
How shall they live?
When the field is tilled
And the wheat is bread
They shall not die in a shortened bed
And a narrow sheet. In this street
There is no beginning, no movement, no peace and
    no end
But noise without speech, food without taste.
Without delay, without haste
We would build the beginning and the end of
    this street.
We build the meaning:
A Church for all
And a job for each
Each man to his work.

II

Thus your fathers were made

Fellow citizens of the saints, of the household
    of GOD, being built upon the foundation

Of apostles and prophets, Christ Jesus Himself
    the chief cornerstone.

But you, have you built well, that you now sit
    helpless in a ruined house?

Where many are born to idleness, to frittered
    lives and squalid deaths, embittered scorn in
    honey-hives,

And those who would build and restore turn out
    the palms of their hands, or look in vain
    towards foreign lands for alms to be more
    or the urn to be filled.

Your building not fitly framed together, you sit
    ashamed and wonder whether and how you
    may be builded together for a habitation of
    GOD in the Spirit, the Spirit which moved
    on the face of the waters like a lantern set
    on the back of a tortoise.

And some say: "How can we love our neigh-
    bour? For love must be made real in act,
    as desire unites with desired; we have only
    our labour to give and our labour is not
    required.

We wait on corners, with nothing to bring but
the songs we can sing which nobody wants
to hear sung;
Waiting to be flung in the end, on a heap less
useful than dung."
You, have you built well, have you forgotten
the cornerstone?
Talking of right relations of men, but not of
relations of men to GOD.
"Our citizenship is in Heaven"; yes, but that is
the model and type for your citizenship
upon earth.

When your fathers fixed the place of GOD,
And settled all the inconvenient saints,
Apostles, martyrs, in a kind of Whipsnade,
Then they could set about imperial expansion
Accompanied by industrial development.
Exporting iron, coal and cotton goods
And intellectual enlightenment
And everything, including capital
And several versions of the Word of GOD:
The British race assured of a mission
Performed it, but left much at home unsure.

Of all that was done in the past, you eat the
fruit, either rotten or ripe.

And the Church must be forever building, and
always decaying, and always being restored.
For every ill deed in the past we suffer the con-
sequence:
For sloth, for avarice, gluttony, neglect of the
Word of GOD,
For pride, for lechery, treachery, for every act of
sin.
And of all that was done that was good, you
have the inheritance.
For good and ill deeds belong to a man alone,
when he stands alone on the other side of
death,
But here upon earth you have the reward of the
good and ill that was done by those who
have gone before you.
And all that is ill you may repair if you walk
together in humble repentance, expiating the
sins of your fathers;
And all that was good you must fight to keep
with hearts as devoted as those of your
fathers who fought to gain it.
The Church must be forever building, for it is
forever decaying within and attacked from
without;
For this is the law of life; and you must re-

member that while there is time of pros-
perity
The people will neglect the Temple, and in time
of adversity they will decry it.

What life have you if you have not life together?
There is no life that is not in community,
And no community not lived in praise of GOD.
Even the anchorite who meditates alone,
For whom the days and nights repeat the praise
of GOD,
Prays for the Church, the Body of Christ incarnate.
And now you live dispersed on ribbon roads,
And no man knows or cares who is his neighbour
Unless his neighbour makes too much disturbance,
But all dash to and fro in motor cars,
Familiar with the roads and settled nowhere.
Nor does the family even move about together,
But every son would have his motor cycle,
And daughters ride away on casual pillions.

Much to cast down, much to build, much to restore;
Let the work not delay, time and the arm not
waste;
Let the clay be dug from the pit, let the saw cut
the stone,
Let the fire not be quenched in the forge.

III

The Word of the LORD came unto me, saying:
O miserable cities of designing men,
O wretched generation of enlightened men,
Betrayed in the mazes of your ingenuities,
Sold by the proceeds of your proper inventions:
I have given you hands which you turn from
    worship,
I have given you speech, for endless palaver,
I have given you my Law, and you set up com-
    missions,
I have given you lips, to express friendly senti-
    ments,
I have given you hearts, for reciprocal distrust.
I have given you power of choice, and you only
    alternate
Between futile speculation and unconsidered ac-
    tion.
Many are engaged in writing books and printing
    them,
Many desire to see their names in print,
Many read nothing but the race reports.
Much is your reading, but not the Word of GOD,
Much is your building, but not the House of GOD.
Will you build me a house of plaster, with cor-
    rugated roofing,
To be filled with a litter of Sunday newspapers?

1ST MALE VOICE:

A Cry from the East:

What shall be done to the shore of smoky ships?

Will you leave my people forgetful and forgotten

To idleness, labour, and delirious stupor?

There shall be left the broken chimney,

The peeled hull, a pile of rusty iron,

In a street of scattered brick where the goat
climbs,

Where My Word is unspoken.

2ND MALE VOICE:

A Cry from the North, from the West and from
the South

Whence thousands travel daily to the timekept
City;

Where My Word is unspoken,

In the land of lobelias and tennis flannels

The rabbit shall burrow and the thorn revisit,

The nettle shall flourish on the gravel court,

And the wind shall say: "Here were decent god-
less people:

Their only monument the asphalt road

And a thousand lost golf balls."

CHORUS:

We build in vain unless the LORD build with us.

Can you keep the City that the LORD keeps not
with you?

A thousand policemen directing the traffic

Cannot tell you why you come or where you go.

A colony of cavies or a horde of active marmots

Build better than they that build without the
LORD.

Shall we lift up our feet among perpetual ruins?

I have loved the beauty of Thy House, the peace
of Thy sanctuary,

I have swept the floors and garnished the altars.

Where there is no temple there shall be no
homes,

Though you have shelters and institutions,

Precarious lodgings while the rent is paid,

Subsiding basements where the rat breeds

Or sanitary dwellings with numbered doors

Or a house a little better than your neighbour's;

When the Stranger says: "What is the meaning
of this city?

Do you huddle close together because you love
each other?"

What will you answer? "We all dwell together

To make money from each other"? or "This is
a community"?

And the Stranger will depart and return to the
    desert.
O my soul, be prepared for the coming of the
    Stranger,
Be prepared for him who knows how to ask
    questions.

O weariness of men who turn from GOD
To the grandeur of your mind and the glory
    of your action,
To arts and inventions and daring enterprises,
To schemes of human greatness thoroughly
    discredited,
Binding the earth and the water to your service,
Exploiting the seas and developing the mountains,
Dividing the stars into common and preferred,
Engaged in devising the perfect refrigerator,
Engaged in working out a rational morality,
Engaged in printing as many books as possible,
Plotting of happiness and flinging empty bottles,
Turning from your vacancy to fevered enthu-
    siasm
For nation or race or what you call humanity;
Though you forget the way to the Temple,
There is one who remembers the way to your
    door:
Life you may evade, but Death you shall not.
You shall not deny the Stranger.

IV

There are those who would build the Temple,
And those who prefer that the Temples should
    not be built.
In the days of Nehemiah the Prophet
There was no exception to the general rule.
In Shushan the palace, in the month Nisan,
He served the wine to the King Artaxerxes,
And he grieved for the broken city, Jerusalem;
And the King gave him leave to depart
That he might rebuild the city.
So he went, with a few, to Jerusalem,
And there, by the dragon's well, by the dung
    gate,
By the fountain gate, by the king's pool,
Jerusalem lay waste, consumed with fire;
No place for a beast to pass.
There were enemies without to destroy him,
And spies and self-seekers within,
When he and his men laid their hands to rebuild-
    ing the wall.
So they built as men must build
With the sword in one hand and the trowel in
    the other.

V

O Lord, deliver me from the man of excellent
    intention and impure heart: for the heart is
    deceitful above all things, and desperately
    wicked.

Sanballat the Horonite and Tobiah the Am-
    monite and Geshem the Arabian: were
    doubtless men of public spirit and zeal.

Preserve me from the enemy who has some-
    thing to gain: and from the friend who has
    something to lose.

Remembering the words of Nehemiah the
    Prophet: "The trowel in hand, and the gun
    rather loose in the holster."

Those who sit in a house of which the use is
    forgotten: are like snakes that lie on moul-
    dering stairs, content in the sunlight.

And the others run about like dogs, full of
    enterprise, sniffing and barking: they say,
    "This house is a nest of serpents, let us
    destroy it,

And have done with these abominations, the
    turpitudes of the Christians." And these are
    not justified, nor the others.

And they write innumerable books; being too
    vain and distracted for silence: seeking every

one after his own elevation, and dodging his emptiness.

If humility and purity be not in the heart, they are not in the home: and if they are not in the home, they are not in the City.

The man who has builded during the day would return to his hearth at nightfall: to be blessed with the gift of silence, and doze before he sleeps.

But we are encompassed with snakes and dogs: therefore some must labour, and others must hold the spears.

VI

It is hard for those who have never known perse-
cution,
And who have never known a Christian,
To believe these tales of Christian persecution.
It is hard for those who live near a Bank
To doubt the security of their money.
It is hard for those who live near a Police Sta-
tion
To believe in the triumph of violence.
Do you think that the Faith has conquered the
World
And that lions no longer need keepers?
Do you need to be told that whatever has been,
can still be?
Do you need to be told that even such modest
attainments
As you can boast in the way of polite society
Will hardly survive the Faith to which they owe
their significance?
Men! polish your teeth on rising and retiring;
Women! polish your fingernails:
You polish the tooth of the dog and the talon
of the cat.
Why should men love the Church? Why should
they love her laws?

She tells them of Life and Death, and of all that
  they would forget.
She is tender where they would be hard, and
  hard where they like to be soft.
She tells them of Evil and Sin, and other un-
  pleasant facts.
They constantly try to escape
From the darkness outside and within
By dreaming of systems so perfect that no one
  will need to be good.
But the man that is will shadow
The man that pretends to be.
And the Son of Man was not crucified once for
  all,
The blood of the martyrs not shed once for all,
The lives of the Saints not given once for all:
But the Son of Man is crucified always
And there shall be Martyrs and Saints.
And if blood of Martyrs is to flow on the steps
We must first build the steps;
And if the Temple is to be cast down
We must first build the Temple.

VII

In the beginning GOD created the world. Waste
    and void. Waste and void. And darkness
    was upon the face of the deep.
And when there were men, in their various
    ways, they struggled in torment towards GOD
Blindly and vainly, for man is a vain thing, and
    man without GOD is a seed upon the wind:
    driven this way and that, and finding no
    place of lodgement and germination.
They followed the light and the shadow, and
    the light led them forward to light and the
    shadow led them to darkness,
Worshipping snakes or trees, worshipping devils
    rather than nothing: crying for life beyond
    life, for ecstasy not of the flesh.
Waste and void. Waste and void. And dark-
    ness on the face of the deep.

And the Spirit moved upon the face of the water.
And men who turned towards the light and were
    known of the light
Invented the Higher Religions; and the Higher
    Religions were good
And led men from light to light, to knowledge
    of Good and Evil.

But their light was ever surrounded and shot
   with darkness
As the air of temperate seas is pierced by the
   still dead breath of the Arctic Current;
And they came to an end, a dead end stirred with
   a flicker of life,
And they came to the withered ancient look of
   a child that has died of starvation.
Prayer wheels, worship of the dead, denial of
   this world, affirmation of rites with forgotten meanings
In the restless wind-whipped sand, or the hills
   where the wind will not let the snow rest.
Waste and void. Waste and void. And darkness on the face of the deep.

Then came, at a predetermined moment, a moment in time and of time,
A moment not out of time, but in time, in what
   we call history: transecting, bisecting the
   world of time, a moment in time but not
   like a moment of time,
A moment in time but time was made through
   that moment: for without the meaning there
   is no time, and that moment of time gave
   the meaning.

Then it seemed as if men must proceed from
    light to light, in the light of the Word,
Through the Passion and Sacrifice saved in spite
    of their negative being;
Bestial as always before, carnal, self-seeking as
    always before, selfish and purblind as ever
    before,
Yet always struggling, always reaffirming, always
    resuming their march on the way that was
    lit by the light;
Often halting, loitering, straying, delaying, re-
    turning, yet following no other way.

But it seems that something has happened that
    has never happened before: though we know
    not just when, or why, or how, or where.
Men have left GOD not for other gods, they say,
    but for no god; and this has never happened
    before
That men both deny gods and worship gods,
    professing first Reason,
And then Money, and Power, and what they call
    Life, or Race, or Dialectic.
The Church disowned, the tower overthrown,
    the bells upturned, what have we to do
But stand with empty hands and palms turned
    upwards

In an age which advances progressively back-
wards?

VOICE OF THE UNEMPLOYED [*afar off*]:
      In this land
There shall be one cigarette to two men,
To two women one half pint of bitter
Ale. . . .

  CHORUS:

What does the world say, does the whole world
    stray in high-powered cars on a by-pass
    way?

VOICE OF THE UNEMPLOYED [*more faintly*]:
      In this land
No man has hired us. . . .

  CHORUS:

Waste and void. Waste and void. And darkness
    on the face of the deep.
Has the Church failed mankind, or has mankind
    failed the Church?
When the Church is no longer regarded, not even
    opposed, and men have forgotten
All gods except Usury, Lust and Power.

VIII

O Father we welcome your words,
And we will take heart for the future,
Remembering the past.

The heathen are come into thine inheritance,
And thy temple have they defiled.

Who is this that cometh from Edom?

He has trodden the wine-press alone.

There came one who spoke of the shame of
    Jerusalem
And the holy places defiled;
Peter the Hermit, scourging with words.
And among his hearers were a few good men,
Many who were evil,
And most who were neither.
Like all men in all places,

Some went from love of glory,
Some went who were restless and curious,
Some were rapacious and lustful.
Many left their bodies to the kites of Syria
Or sea-strewn along the routes;

Many left their souls in Syria,
Living on, sunken in moral corruption;
Many came back well broken,
Diseased and beggared, finding
A stranger at the door in possession:
Came home cracked by the sun of the East
And the seven deadly sins in Syria.

But our King did well at Acre.
And in spite of all the dishonour,
The broken standards, the broken lives,
The broken faith in one place or another,
There was something left that was more than the
     tales
Of old men on winter evenings.
Only the faith could have done what was good
     of it,
Whole faith of a few,
Part faith of many.
Not avarice, lechery, treachery,
Envy, sloth, gluttony, jealousy, pride:
It was not these that made the Crusades,
But these that unmade them.

Remember the faith that took men from home
At the call of a wandering preacher.

Our age is an age of moderate virtue
And of moderate vice
When men will not lay down the Cross
Because they will never assume it.
Yet nothing is impossible, nothing,
To men of faith and conviction.
Let us therefore make perfect our will.
O GOD, help us.

IX

Son of Man, behold with thine eyes, and hear
with thine ears
And set thine heart upon all that I show thee.
Who is this that has said: the House of GOD is
a House of Sorrow;
We must walk in black and go sadly, with long-
drawn faces,
We must go between empty walls, quavering
lowly, whispering faintly,
Among a few flickering scattered lights?
They would put upon GOD their own sorrow,
the grief they should feel
For their sins and faults as they go about their
daily occasions.
Yet they walk in the street proudnecked, like
thoroughbreds ready for races,
Adorning themselves, and busy in the market,
the forum,
And all other secular meetings.
Thinking good of themselves, ready for any fes-
tivity,
Doing themselves very well.
Let us mourn in a private chamber, learning the
way of penitence,
And then let us learn the joyful communion of
saints.

The soul of Man must quicken to creation.

Out of the formless stone, when the artist united
himself with stone,

Spring always new forms of life, from the soul
of man that is joined to the soul of stone;

Out of the meaningless practical shapes of all
that is living or lifeless

Joined with the artist's eye, new life, new form,
new colour.

Out of the sea of sound the life of music,

Out of the slimy mud of words, out of the sleet
and hail of verbal imprecisions,

Approximate thoughts and feelings, words that
have taken the place of thoughts and feelings,

There spring the perfect order of speech, and the
beauty of incantation.

LORD, shall we not bring these gifts to Your service?

Shall we not bring to Your service all our powers

For life, for dignity, grace and order,

And intellectual pleasures of the senses?

The LORD who created must wish us to create

And employ our creation again in His service

Which is already His service in creating.

For Man is joined spirit and body,

And therefore must serve as spirit and body.
Visible and invisible, two worlds meet in Man;
Visible and invisible must meet in His Temple;
You must not deny the body.

Now you shall see the Temple completed:
After much striving, after many obstacles;
For the work of creation is never without travail;
The formed stone, the visible crucifix,
The dressed altar, the lifting light,

Light

Light

The visible reminder of Invisible Light.

X

You have seen the house built, you have seen it
　　adorned

By one who came in the night, it is now dedicated
　　to GOD.

It is now a visible church, one more light set on a
　　hill

In a world confused and dark and disturbed by
　　portents of fear.

And what shall we say of the future? Is one
　　church all we can build?

Or shall the Visible Church go on to conquer the
　　World?

The great snake lies ever half awake, at the bot-
　　tom of the pit of the world, curled

In folds of himself until he awakens in hunger
　　and moving his head to right and to left
　　prepares for his hour to devour.

But the Mystery of Iniquity is a pit too deep for
　　mortal eyes to plumb. Come

Ye out from among those who prize the serpent's
　　golden eyes,

The worshippers, self-given sacrifice of the
　　snake. Take

Your way and be ye separate.

Be not too curious of Good and Evil;
Seek not to count the future waves of Time;
But be ye satisfied that you have light
Enough to take your step and find your foothold.

O Light Invisible, we praise Thee!
Too bright for mortal vision.
O Greater Light, we praise Thee for the less;
The eastern light our spires touch at morning,
The light that slants upon our western doors at
    evening,
The twilight over stagnant pools at batflight,
Moon light and star light, owl and moth light,
Glow-worm glowlight on a grassblade.
O Light Invisible, we worship Thee!

We thank Thee for the lights that we have
    kindled,
The light of altar and of sanctuary;
Small lights of those who meditate at midnight
And lights directed through the coloured panes
    of windows
And light reflected from the polished stone,
The gilded carven wood, the coloured fresco.
Our gaze is submarine, our eyes look upward
 And see the light that fractures through unquiet
    water.

We see the light but see not whence it comes.
O Light Invisible, we glorify Thee!

In our rhythm of earthly life we tire of light.
We are glad when the day ends, when the
play ends; and ecstasy is too much pain.
We are children quickly tired: children who are
up in the night and fall asleep as the rocket
is fired; and the day is long for work or play.
We tire of distraction or concentration, we sleep
and are glad to sleep,
Controlled by the rhythm of blood and the day
and the night and the seasons.
And we must extinguish the candle, put out the
light and relight it;
Forever must quench, forever relight the flame.
Therefore we thank Thee for our little light, that
is dappled with shadow.
We thank Thee who hast moved us to building,
to finding, to forming at the ends of our
fingers and beams of our eyes.
And when we have built an altar to the Invisible
Light, we may set thereon the little lights
for which our bodily vision is made.
And we thank Thee that darkness reminds us of
light.
O Light Invisible, we give Thee thanks for Thy
great glory!

BURNT NORTON

τοῦ λόγου δ'ἐόντος ξυνοῦ ζώουσιν οἱ πολλοὶ
ὡς ἰδίαν ἔχοντες φρόνησιν.

I. p. 77. Fr. 2.

ὁδὸς ἄνω κάτω μία καὶ ωὐτή.

I. p. 89. Fr. 60.

Diels: *Die Fragmente der Vorsokratiker* (Herakleitos).

I

TIME present and time past
Are both perhaps present in time future,
And time future contained in time past.
If all time is eternally present
All time is unredeemable.
What might have been is an abstraction
Remaining a perpetual possibility
Only in a world of speculation.
What might have been and what has been
Point to one end, which is always present.
Footfalls echo in the memory
Down the passage which we did not take
Towards the door we never opened
Into the rose-garden. My words echo
Thus, in your mind.
                    But to what purpose
Disturbing the dust on a bowl of rose-leaves
I do not know.
                    Other echoes
Inhabit the garden. Shall we follow?
Quick, said the bird, find them, find them,
Round the corner. Through the first gate,
Into our first world, shall we follow
The deception of the thrush? Into our first world.
There they were, dignified, invisible,

Moving without pressure, over the dead leaves,
In the autumn heat, through the vibrant air,
And the bird called, in response to
The unheard music hidden in the shrubbery,
And the unseen eyebeam crossed, for the roses
Had the look of flowers that are looked at.
There they were as our guests, accepted and ac-
cepting.
So we moved, and they, in a formal pattern,
Along the empty alley, into the box circle,
To look down into the drained pool.
Dry the pool, dry concrete, brown edged,
And the pool was filled with water out of sunlight,
And the lotos rose, quietly, quietly,
The surface glittered out of heart of light,
And they were behind us, reflected in the pool.
Then a cloud passed, and the pool was empty.
Go, said the bird, for the leaves were full of chil-
dren,
Hidden excitedly, containing laughter.
Go, go, go, said the bird: human kind
Cannot bear very much reality.
Time past and time future
What might have been and what has been
Point to one end, which is always present.

II

Garlic and sapphires in the mud
Clot the bedded axle-tree.
The trilling wire in the blood
Sings below inveterate scars
And reconciles forgotten wars.
The dance along the artery
The circulation of the lymph
Are figured in the drift of stars
Ascend to summer in the tree
We move above the moving tree
In light upon the figured leaf
And hear upon the sodden floor
Below, the boarhound and the boar
Pursue their pattern as before
But reconciled among the stars.

At the still point of the turning world. Neither
    flesh nor fleshless;
Neither from nor towards; at the still point, there
    the dance is,
But neither arrest nor movement. And do not
    call it fixity.
Where past and future are gathered. Neither move-
    ment from nor towards,
Neither ascent nor decline. Except for the point,
    the still point,

There would be no dance, and there is only the
    dance.
I can only say, *there* we have been: but I cannot
    say where.
And I cannot say, how long, for that is to place
    it in time.

The inner freedom from the practical desire,
The release from action and suffering, release from
    the inner
And the outer compulsion, yet surrounded
By a grace of sense, a white light still and moving,
Erhebung without motion, concentration
Without elimination, both a new world
And the old made explicit, understood
In the completion of its partial ecstasy,
The resolution of its partial horror.
Yet the enchainment of past and future
Woven in the weakness of the changing body,
Protects mankind from heaven and damnation
Which flesh cannot endure.
                              Time past and time future
Allow but a little consciousness.
To be conscious is not to be in time
But only in time can the moment in the rose-garden,
The moment in the arbour where the rain beat,

The moment in the draughty church at smoke-
    fall
Be remembered; involved with past and future.
Only through time time is conquered.

III

Here is a place of disaffection
Time before and time after
In a dim light: neither daylight
Investing form with lucid stillness
Turning shadow into transient beauty
With slow rotation suggesting permanence
Nor darkness to purify the soul
Emptying the sensual with deprivation
Cleansing affection from the temporal.
Neither plenitude nor vacancy. Only a flicker
Over the strained time-ridden faces
Distracted from distraction by distraction
Filled with fancies and empty of meaning
Tumid apathy with no concentration
Men and bits of paper, whirled by the cold wind
That blows before and after time,
Wind in and out of unwholesome lungs
Time before and time after.
Eructation of unhealthy souls
Into the faded air, the torpid

Driven on the wind that sweeps the gloomy hills
        of London,
Hampstead and Clerkenwell, Campden and Putney,
Highgate, Primrose and Ludgate. Not here
Not here the darkness, in this twittering world.

Descend lower, descend only
Into the world of perpetual solitude,
World not world, but that which is not world,
Internal darkness, deprivation
And destitution of all property,
Dessication of the world of sense,
Evacuation of the world of fancy,
Inoperancy of the world of spirit;
This is the one way, and the other
Is the same, not in movement
But abstention from movement; while the world
        moves
In appetency, on its metalled ways
Of time past and time future.

IV

Time and the bell have buried the day,
The black cloud carries the sun away.
Will the sunflower turn to us, will the clematis
Stray down, bend to us; tendril and spray

Clutch and cling?
Chill
Fingers of yew be curled
Down on us? After the kingfisher's wing
Has answered light to light, and is silent, the light
  is still
At the still point of the turning world.

V

Words move, music moves
Only in time; but that which is only living
Can only die. Words, after speech, reach
Into the silence. Only by the form, the pattern,
Can words or music reach
The stillness, as a Chinese jar still
Moves perpetually in its stillness.
Not the stillness of the violin, while the note lasts,
Not that only, but the co-existence,
Or say that the end precedes the beginning,
And the end and the beginning were always there
Before the beginning and after the end.
And all is always now. Words strain,
Crack and sometimes break, under the burden,
Under the tension, slip, slide, perish,
Decay with imprecision, will not stay in place,
Will not stay still. Shrieking voices

Scolding, mocking, or merely chattering,
Always assail them. The Word in the desert
Is most attacked by voices of temptation,
The crying shadow in the funeral dance,
The loud lament of the disconsolate chimera.

The detail of the pattern is movement,
As in the figure of the ten stairs.
Desire itself is movement
Not in itself desirable;
Love is itself unmoving,
Only the cause and end of movement,
Timeless, and undesiring
Except in the aspect of time
Caught in the form of limitation
Between un-being and being.
Sudden in a shaft of sunlight
Even while the dust moves
There rises the hidden laughter
Of children in the foliage
Quick now, here, now, always—
Ridiculous the waste sad time
Stretching before and after.